*To Edward
Love & Light on your path
Diane
6/15/01*

441 736 2226

Diane Tessman

SEVEN RAYS OF
THE
HEALING MILLENNIUM

INNER LIGHT PUBLICATIONS
NEW BRUNSWICK, NJ

SEVEN RAYS
OF THE
HEALING MILLENNIUM

ISBN: 0-938294-74-1

MANUFACTURED IN THE UNITED STATES OF AMERICA

Editorial Direction:
Timothy Green Beckley

Inside Art:
Lynn Kvistad, Merrilee Miller, Carol Ann Rodriguez, Pat A. Davey

Composition, layout & design:
Eye Scry Designs, Yucca Valley, California

For permission to reprint specific portions or to inquire about foreign rights:

Inner Light
PO Box 753
New Brunswick, NJ 08903

Free catalogue of books upon request

SEVEN RAYS OF HEALING MILLENNIUM

Table of Contents

SEVEN RAYS OF HEALING MILLENNIUM

Table of Contents

INTRODUCTION:
WHO IS DIANE TESSMAN?

In its Spring, 1997 issue, **Unsolved UFO Sightings** magazine features an article entitled "Diane Tessman: Prophet of the New Age," and speaks of Diane as "one of the leading voices in the rising chorus of seekers of enlightenment," at the close of the millennium.

"An entire culture has grown up around this phenomenon of 'channeling,' a movement of forward-looking, life-affirming mysticism called 'The New Age,'" and eminent among this movement is "gifted writer and psychic Diane Tessman," writes Sean Casteel, author of the feature.

Diane Tessman remains a leader of the New Age after fifteen amazing years as a channel and writer; she has more than lived up to Ruth Montgomery's original insightful endorsement in her book, **Aliens Among Us,** in which Ruth identifies Diane as a true star person. In reference to Diane and her channeling ability, Ruth's guides told her, "...space people are indeed able to contact through mental telepathy, those who are open in their vibrations and take time for meditation, which is a way to hear unspoken words. (Diane's) contact is real, Ruth."

While teaching school in the 1970s, Diane joined MUFON (the Mutual UFO Network), researching and investigating UFO sightings, encounters, and abductions. However, Diane knew within herself that her motivation for looking into UFO and paranormal phenomena was more than idle curiosity. She suspected that she had experienced an alien encounter when she was a child on a North Iowa farm.

This suspicion was confirmed in 1981 when Diane underwent hypnosis with Dr. R. Leo Sprinkle, Ph.D., professor at the University of Wyoming (now retired), and noted psychologist. Dr. Sprinkle soon became convinced that Diane's memories were "real," and that "they have a profound influence on her inner character and personal goals."

In this hypnosis, Diane remembered being taken aboard a UFO twice when she was very young. Although she remembered many details of the beings on board the starship as well as details of the ships themselves, by far the most outstanding aspect of her encounters were her visits with a human-looking being called "Tibus."

The details of Diane's two UFO experiences, including Dr. Sprinkle's notes during and after her hypnosis, can be found in Diane's first book entitled, **The Transformation**. Also in **The Transformation** are accounts of the many paranormal events which began occurring around Diane's Florida home in the early 1980s, and Tibus' first channeled messages to the people of Earth.

A year after her memories were jogged through Dr. Sprinkle's hypnotic regression, Diane began to receive telepathic messages from this being called Tibus. At the same time, Diane began a new career as a professional psychic counselor; Diane blended her own psychic ability with Tibus' channeled in-put in order to give her clients warnings, insights, guidance, and new hope regarding their lives. Word soon spread regarding Diane's accuracy in spiritual and psychic readings, and she became a leading counselor in great demand in the San Diego area where she had moved in 1981.

However, Tibus' telepathic guidance was for Diane to turn to written channeled messages which urgently needed to reach people all over the globe. He explained that he and others in his Space/Time Intelligence needed to send these vital transmissions to specific individuals through Diane, and it must be done, "Now!"

These messages concerned the fact that some individuals are "star people" (enlightened humans), and that they must now awaken and lead the human race into a new, higher level of consciousness. Tibus told Diane that the human race has to take a step in spiritual evolution almost overnight, or become extinct. He stressed that Earth is a living entity and that humankind has done immense damage to their Mother World.

"Humans must wake up, stop destroying the planet they stand on, and begin to cherish her; all this must be done just as the millennium changes!" Tibus admonishes.

Tibus told Diane back in 1983 that "The Change Times" will begin to occur in the 1990s, and that huge, sweeping, often violent Earth Changes will soon be here."

In fact, Tibus predicted much which has already happened, from global warming to increased volcanic activity to mutated viruses which threaten the entire world.

"Earth will never be the same again, but we can make this a better reality instead of waiting for Doomsday, Diane, but we must reach many humans and their frequency of consciousness in order to do this!"

In 1983, Diane therefore began **The Star Network Heartline**

Newsletter which has run steadily each month since then. Now in its fifteenth year, **The Heartline** is a beacon of hope to enlightened people across the globe, with monthly predictions and urgent messages from Tibus as well as orchestrated Cleansing/Healing Days in which the readership prays and meditates in an effort to raise the spiritual frequency of humankind, and save the dying planet.

The Change Times Quarterly is published four times a year by Diane, with channeled messages from a number of astounding beings from the higher dimensions who send urgent transmissions for the readership as the Change Times progress in an often frightening manner.

In 1995, Diane wrote her second major book for Inner Light Publishing entitled, **Earth Changes Bible.** She is also co-author of the book, **Your Passport to Heaven,** with Timothy Green Beckley.

Diane has lived in St. Thomas, U.S. Virgin Islands, and the Republic of Ireland, as well as Iowa, Florida, The Netherlands, and California. Her five year experience in Ireland is particularly dear to her; there she studied ancient Celt shamanism and had many fascinating, other-worldly experiences.

It was in Ireland that she established contact with the interdimensional tribe who call themselves, The Tuatha De Danann, or The Family of Diane. These ancient people were early settlers in Ireland who were said to have come from the sky. They "turned sideways to the sun," (became other-dimensional), when they became disgusted with humanity's greed and cruelty. Diane cherishes her contact with The Tuatha De Danann in particular because they are from another dimension of Earth rather than from space. Diane feels strongly that in the New Age, we must learn to value Earth beings as much as beings from far distant planets.

Upon her return from Ireland, Diane lived in Joshua Tree, California, and researched George van Tassel's famous Giant Rock and Integratron. California's High Desert was the birthplace of modern UFO contact and telepathic channeling, and remains an extremely active location for UFO encounters and sightings today.

Diane was honored to be guest speaker at Denver, Palm Springs, and Phoenix UFO/New Age Conferences in 1995, and was featured on the front page of Palm Springs' **Desert Sun** newspaper.

1997 has been a red letter year, because Diane was able to return to the exact location of her early childhood UFO encounters: the North Iowa farm.

This piece of land abounds with nature spirits and voices from other dimensions; Diane had known this in her childhood but, being a child, had not been able to analyze it. Now, through a miracle, she has been able to move back to this magical land, and can experience and enjoy its many delightful strangenesses as well as analyzing "what and why." It is as if her life is beginning all over again!

Diane lives on 10.27 acres in North Iowa and runs an animal shelter when not writing, channeling, or hiking through the woods to the river; her "shelter" friends soon become members of her (large) household. Diane loves nature and its animals, and is active in environmental and animal rights causes. She firmly believes in activism as well as spiritual and psychic power, in order to raise the human frequency.

Her "star guardian" Tibus, whom she encountered in her childhood on the same land, has remained with Diane throughout the years. His

Tibus' direct telepathic input to Diane is caught on film

channeled messages abound with humor and wisdom, and he is much-loved by Diane's many readers and friends. Details on Tibus' origin and philosophy are given at the close of "The Prelude from Tibus."

Diane and Tibus hope that you will benefit from their new **Seven Rays of the Healing Millennium**; "hope" is the most precious force in the universe, and we hope this miraculous "stuff" will be found by you within these pages. It is never too late. Let's go together into The Healing Millennium which lies before us.

PRELUDE: THE PRECIOUS SYMBOL OF THE CRYSTAL CROSS

Just before my career as a channel and counselor began in 1982, I found a tiny but exquisite crystal cross in the back yard of my rented home near San Diego, California. As I picked it up, I knew intuitively that my life would never be the same again. "This means something, something wonderful!" I said to myself.

On the day I found the little crystal cross, my life was in a downward spiral. I could not find a teaching position in California, no matter how hard I tried; not even a substitute job was available. I had moved to California with my young daughter and my animal friends after teaching for eleven years in The Virgin Islands and Florida. Living expenses in California were very high and I simply was not making it.

I worked part time at K-Mart for minimum wage, attempted to be a secretary for a large insurance firm but got fired for telling their customers the truth regarding details of their policies, and finally, I had applied for welfare payments. Never in the world had I imagined I'd be asking for welfare!

From the moment I found The Crystal Cross, my life changed. My channeling ability blossomed in my conscious mind so that I could access it (and Tibus), at will; I began receiving astounding messages from Tibus, the being whom I had encountered as a child on the Iowa farm. I then began my career as a counselor and channel with the help of Timothy Green Beckley of Inner Light Publishing.

*I purchased an ancient typewriter at a garage sale and began typing my first book for Inner Light, **The Transformation**. Also, I was suddenly very much in demand around San Diego as a psychic reader and counselor. On top of this, I began receiving written requests for channeled counseling from all over the world. I appeared as featured guest at major UFO conferences and was the guest on radio and television shows. I then purchased my own house in Southern California, only six months after finding the tiny Crystal Cross. I could not believe I had been on welfare without any real hope, just six months before! The Crystal Cross was indeed the powerful symbol of my life's transformation.*

As you meditate with the Crystal Cross, remember that the Crystal Cross glistens with the seven colorful rays of the spectrum: Red, Orange, Yellow, Green, Blue, Indigo, and Violet. Allow The Crystal Cross to catch the sun's light and channel its prism effect into the healing colors of the rainbow for you.

As well as being the powerful symbol of Christian belief, The Cross is also an ancient symbol from pre-Christian times representing the crossing of The Four Directions. Today, we should be concentrating on the ley lines which crisscross Mother Earth. These are the energy rivers of her psychic force; we need to work with these ley lines as we pray to heal the planet from the damage Man has done to her. The symbol of "the crystal, crossing" is therefore a powerful meditative helper as you work with Earth's ley energies.

Channeled energy swirls around Diane's head

The Mother Planet uses this "crystal crossing" combination extensively as she creates her wondrous reality: The Four Seasons, The Four Winds, The Four Elements, and The Four Phases of the Moon are a few examples of this. Later in the book, we have channeled information regarding these which can be used in powerful meditations.

I am thrilled to have The Crystal Cross as the symbol of this book. It has been a magnificent symbol of good fortune and enlightenment within my own life, and I know that its power can touch all who discover its sacred beauty.

Diane Tessman
P.O. Box 352
St. Ansgar, Iowa 50472

CHAPTER ONE:
FROM TIBUS, THE FIRST STEP IN THE BLUEPRINT

This is Tibus. I come to you in love and light.

The truth is out there. But, can we ever bring it into our own lives? Can we bring it from "out there" to "in here," and know beyond a shadow of a doubt, that the truth is now within our minds, our hearts, and our souls?

The answer is, "Yes!"

In the new millennium which stretches before us, we will finally have–truth! Blatant lies which are thousands of years old, will die, and release us from our dark prison.

Through the darkness of thousands of years, there will shine a beam of light. That light is the light of truth. Once that light manifests, the darkness which has plagued the (human) race and its world for countless years, will be no more. To use a "Star Wars" term, the human race will move from answering to the Dark Side of The Force, to embracing the Light Side.

Why do we know the light will shine through the dark night of the human soul? Because this is the absolute truth of the coming millennium. We call it, The Healing Millennium.

It is a foregone reality that the light will shine. Just as you know there will be light in the morning, you must now know that the light of truth will dawn in the coming millennium. It is a cycle, it is the way of the universe. The light of the Healing Millennium is as certain to happen as is the light of dawn in tomorrow's morning sky.

Allow us to define "the darkness of the human soul" of which we speak: It is the darkness of brutality, violence, greed, insensitivity, and injustice which is currently thriving all over the planet. We speak of man's inhumanity to man, man's inhumanity to his world (the environment), and man's inhumanity to his own soul.

Few people on Earth at this moment comprehend that we will be entering a new phase of the cosmic wheel when we move into The Year 2000, and beyond. This new phase is so dramatically different from the old phase, that it really must be called, a whole new dimension.

This dimension is one which will heal the human mind of its brutality, heal the human soul of its greed, and heal the human heart of its hatred.

Why? Because all of us are, in truth, particles of consciousness within the Mind of God, and the Mind of God is turning, ever turning, without fail, toward a new dawn, a new dimension.

The great revolving cosmic wheel is the Creator Spirit's soul, and within this soul, we all dwell. You are a molecule of this Creator Spirit.

In the year 2000 and beyond, the Great Wheel will have rolled into a brand new intersect point of space/time, just as certainly as Earth revolves into the morning.

The only key which you must have in order to be a part of this new dimension of light and truth, is to have the awareness to know you are there!

If you are an animal lover, you have tried to save a stray puppy or kitten at some point in your life. You want so much for that poor, frightened, hungry, animal to realize that you are trying to save it. But often, it does not realize, it just isn't aware. And, as you try to coax it closer with food, it gets desperately scared of some little noise, and it runs away.

Hopefully, you have had a successful effort or two as well, and a once frightened, hungry puppy is now your devoted, loving, dog friend.

Why did you manage to save your dog friend but not some other frightened little stray which you never saw again? Because your dog friend was aware "enough." He realized, finally, when he was a stray, that you were trying to save him.

In the same way, you must be aware of what is happening. You must be aware of the beautiful light, the magnificent truth, which stretches before us in the Healing Millennium. You must not be afraid to reach out at this time!

Otherwise, this new dimension will be like a radio station which you don't realize you should tune into. It will broadcast its frequency, but you will not receive it. You must be aware of "that spot on the dial," and seek that frequency of feeling, thinking, and being.

The coming Healing Millennium is a difficult reality to explain in words. How would you describe the dawn's first light to an individual who had been locked in a dark prison for fifty years?
He might have a vague memory of the beauty and truth of the light of day, but he would need a bit of counseling and advice before he raced out into the dawn's first rays. So it is with the human race, and so we offer counsel.

Many books offer counsel or a description of "what the New Age will be like." But we have found what is most needed is a workable glue to bring it all—together. In this book, we will give that glue.

Until now, each voice of the New Age has tended to have its own terminology, its own version of events, its own spiritual analysis of aliens, its own psychic philosophy. But the minutes are ticking, the new millennium approaches. We must find real and true direction to all the strangeness, and we must find it now!

Finding the real and true direction is the only way you will become aware "enough" to tune into the new dawn as it manifests on the planet. This is the only way you will no longer be the victim of corporate and governmental injustice, society's insensitivity, cover-ups, lies, and conspiracies. This is the only way you will escape the slavery to which the current "money system" subjects you.

My empathy with your situation is very great. For all intent and purposes, I am you, a citizen of Earth at the end of a dark millennium. In the same way, you must become me, a human of the new dawn, a citizen of the Healing Millennium.

You personally are the bridge to the planet's future as well as the bridge to your own positive future.

Consider the sand on the beach as yet unformed, which is just waiting for you to build a great sand castle. So it is with the "molecules of creation" which compose your future, and the entire future human consciousness. The future is sheer magic, my friends; it can be anything!

You personally are also an alien. You are alien to the low frequency of the modern world. You do not know how to trample others in order to get ahead yourself, but you see others doing this and feel great despair. You are true to your inner guidance, knowing that there is great promise in the human potential, but you perceive just the opposite in the modern world.

Yes, you feel like an alien in this time and place, yet you keep an ancient, magical, mystical thing called - hope.

Hope is everything, it is the molecules of the future consciousness. Never stop hoping; I promise you, your hopes and dreams for this planet and its people will become reality.

Often we advise our friends to consider their past lives as the many slices of a whole pie. In this way, it can be perceived that past lives are actually lifetimes occurring simultaneously with the present lifetime. They are parallel aspects (slices) of the whole pie - the Whole You. Your present lifetime is also "just a slice" of the Whole You. Another term for the Whole You is the Higher Self.

We also perceive The Seven Rays of human consciousness which compose the Whole You; this spiritually evolved human being will be able to face the new dawn of the Healing Millennium with wonder, joy and confidence.

If the individual has not become consciously whole, has not found profound direction, and the "glue" of higher awareness, he or she will be left behind in the low frequency of the old dark millennium.

However, the old millennium is dying. The old dimension will soon unravel into oblivion and extinction, and with, it will go those who could not spiritually evolve.

Join us now as we explore and explain The Seven Rays of Consciousness which compose the Future You and which lead into the Healing Millennium.

These are the keys to the future human consciousness; these are the keys to your personal future.

May the healing light of Goodness surround you always,
Tibus

WHO IS TIBUS? A NOTE ON TIBUS' INDENTITY

Tibus is a being of Space and Time who began sending telepathic messages to Diane Tessman in the early 1980s. However, Diane feels she has known him all her life, because it was Tibus whom she met during her childhood UFO encounters. These encounters are detailed in her first book, **The Transformation** published by Inner Light, and still available from Diane personally.

Tibus describes himself as a "future human" rather than a space alien from a distant planet circling a distant sun. He explains that he is of the future human consciousness, not the present human consciousness. He has traveled back to us, through time, to help us into the future and away from Doomsday.

Tibus also explains that the dimension of time has remained a mystery to humankind for thousands of dark years, but in the coming Healing Millennium, we as human beings will be able to completely comprehend "time" (or the lack thereof).

What is more exciting, we will be able to overcome time itself. We will no longer be imprisoned at a particular point in human history. We will be able to travel through "time."

There is a stipulation, however: first, we must evolve spiritually. If a being is not sufficiently evolved, he or she will not survive becoming a being of "timelessness."

Where/when Tibus comes from, humans can and do travel the dimension of time, they are not chained to "time." We can know, then, that we made it because Tibus and his brethren are, simply put, our children's children.

Tibus continues to explain his home source by saying that humans also travel in outer space in his future dimension, associating successfully with various kinds of aliens throughout the galaxy.

In the future, the human race will have grown up; we are to become cosmic citizens, not citizens of one world or one timeframe. We are evolving from Homo sapiens to Homo cosmos!

For fifteen years, Diane and Tibus have sent their monthly newsletter, **The Star Network Heartline**, to thousands of readers. Diane has realized over the years, that Tibus has a very definite plan, a blueprint, which is guiding those humans who read his messages through very troubled times of change.

This amazes Diane, because she did not realize for many years that there was an overview or a plan; she merely knew she was supposed to get Tibus' messages to her fellow human beings.

The closer we move to the new millennium, the more Diane realizes that Tibus has a very specific plan for helping his fellow humans into the future.

Tibus is the voice of the future human consciousness. We know that we did make it into a very beautiful future, because Tibus exists as a flesh and blood human being, from that future. He reaches back to help us leap into that future. What promise awaits us!

CHAPTER TWO:
A BRIEF OVERVIEW OF THE SITUATION

As the change of millennia draws near, we live in a world of inner and outer confusion:

What is the truth about a flying saucer crash at Roswell, New Mexico, in 1947, and are there aliens from outer space visiting us? What is the truth about social security? Will it be there for the "baby boomers" or did we, in good faith, pay into our country's retirement system for nothing? Were we robbed? Where did our money go? What will we do?

What is the truth about the horrendous, deadly Ebola virus, and other mutated, horrible viruses? Are viruses about to take the next logical step, and explode into the civilized world, decimating billions of people and other life forms?

Are the immune systems of higher mammals, including humans, deteriorating? Is this the truth about how Mother Earth plans to get rid of the (human) species? Humans are the most grossly overpopulated animal on the face of Earth.

What is the truth about the rumors that the United States is headed for a second revolution in which "Ruby Ridge" and "Remember Waco" will be the battle cries?

Is the United States going to fall apart with Texas becoming Hispanic, Idaho becoming white separatist, and goodness knows what the rest of us will be?

We want to know the truth about angels, entities, and beings from other worlds and dimensions: In our childhood, organized religion taught us that angels were "out there" but that we were going too far if we actually saw and communicated with them, ourselves. Now we suspect that angels and other beings have always been accessible to us personally and we are tired of religion denying us direct access to our higher beings.

And, what religion are those UFO occupants?

What is the truth about the Larsen Ice Shelf and the entire Antarctic? Are they really melting as fast as they say? Is the ice cap of Mt. Fuji melting? Where is all that water going? It is, after all, more water than we can even comprehend, and it is pouring into the oceans every second. Earth's oceans grow warmer and warmer.

The Earth will very soon no longer have weighty chunks of ice at her Southern and Northern Polar Caps, so will the lack of weight at the all-important poles knock the revolving globe off balance?

What is the truth about our world's climate these days? It is changing dramatically and rapidly. There are more violent storms, floods, fires. Volcanoes are firing all over, and earthquakes are rumbling almost constantly now.

You can find the clear truth about these questions and a thousand other modern concerns and crisis, through knowledge of "The Seven Rays," ancient and mystical, which blend together within you to form your Whole Self. Knowledge of the Seven Rays is power!

Incidentally, we wish to capitalize "Whole Self" because this form of you will be greater, more complete, than the fragmented you. Your Whole Self is the evolved you. Your Whole Self is your Higher Self.

We as a human race have been fragmented in our perception of the universe for a long and dark time. It is time to become Whole. Then the truth will be yours.

© 1997 KVISTAD

Is this compassionate alien the same race as the aliens killed at Roswell?

Artist: Lynn Kvistad

18

CHAPTER THREE:
THE WHOLE YOU

At this stage in our human evolution, we use either the left side of our brain to complete a task or solve a problem, or we use the right side.

Science tells us that the left side of the brain provides logic and practicality while the right side provides intuition and spirituality.

The phenomenon of unidentified flying objects (UFOs) gives us an example of how we as a human race attempt to solve a puzzle for which we honestly have no immediate answer.

Looking at a UFO with the left side of the self, we wonder what degree of arc the object is in the sky, how big it appears compared to the moon, or to a nearby house, what colors emanate from it, in what order, and the precise amount of time it hovers in a stationary position.

Looking at a UFO with the right side of the self, we feel an overwhelming sense of awe, we have the feeling we are being watched by someone or something inside the UFO, we "know" it is a solid craft, and we "know" this craft is "absolutely huge," but we have no real proof of this.

The truth about what the UFO really is, its origin, its size, who is inside it, and what their mission here really is, is a truth which takes the Whole Self to comprehend. We stand on the brink of being able to perceive as the Whole Self as the Dark Millennium draws to a close.

Logic and practicality alone cannot give the full picture, nor can intuition and spirituality. And so, the human race has been a race divided from within for many millennia.

We feel a primal attraction to something we call mysticism. Mysticism is the cousin of spirituality and intuition. It includes religious needs, superstition, and psychic feelings and curiosity.

From the other half of our Whole, we feel an attraction to scientific thought and procedure, we want to have a level head on our collective shoulders, and we want to be intellectually proficient without listening to superstition, intuition, or spiritual whims. We worship technology.

No wonder our race is confused!

At the end of the 20th Century, we can look back and admit, we as an entire race, are schizophrenic.

The tragic aspect is, we have brought not only ourselves but our entire planet, with its millions of magnificent life forms, to the brink of disaster and extinction with our confusion. This is where our half-brain perception has gotten us.

For example, our scientific nature led us to be desperately curious about splitting the atom. Our logic and intellect enabled us to find the secret of splitting the atom, and, of course, we did so.

Then the spiritual side of us cried out, "People are dying from this radiation! We could wipe out all life on the planet. We must stop splitting the atom!"

Next, the dark side of our spiritual sense was reached when we were told that we must hate "Red Communists" with a superstitious, blind, primitive hatred, and that they were about to drop the atom bomb on the western side of the world.

Finally, our two halves merged and said with logical yet spiritual enlightenment, "This nuclear stuff is really dangerous! Forget the blind hatred taught during the Cold War. We as the entire human race need to get this under control!"

This example illustrates that the schizophrenia of the human race is not a simple thing. There is a dark side to both science (the left brain), and spirituality (the right brain). Luckily, there is a light side to each of these as well.

Throughout our history, we have taken two steps forward and three steps backward, thanks to our mental and spiritual confusion as a race.

We go to war in the name of religion and then we bravely try to heal the badly wounded enemy soldier, also in the name of religion. Our Christian charity and our righteous wrath are all mixed together, yet we seem able to perceive only one side of the coin at a given moment.

In this one sided perception, the real and complete truth is almost always lost.

Now, as the new millennium approaches, we as a human race are about to take a major step in evolution.

Not every individual within the human race will be able to take this step, but some will. In the overview, it is the entire race which is evolving; those left behind will be the "rejects" of this evolutionary process. Sadly, this is true of every evolutionary process: Those who cannot "reach" are left behind.

Evolution, just like God, works in mysterious ways, and it is impossible to say how many will be able to take the step up the evolutionary ladder. Sometimes it is just one or two members of a species who are able to take the next step and become the "Adam and Eve" of a new species.

In other evolutionary steps, millions of members of a species have evolved at about the same time.

The Creator Spirit does not seem to care how many of a species jump on board as an evolutionary step is taken. The universal creative process seems only to care that change does take place, and that some members of a species make it aboard.

It is fascinating to note, scientists have recently determined that the process of evolution does not necessarily inch its way along as we originally thought, taking thousands or millions of years. No, it seems that evolution has happened almost overnight to a number of species throughout history.

The evolutionary process which is currently working on and within the human race, is one which also seems to be happening "overnight," although it has been building for thousands of years. Although the process had been evolving in a hidden fashion for thousands of years, it took one micro-second for the ape-person to finally pick up the bone as a tool. And, the world has never been the same since. Now, we stand on a new precipice.

Unluckily, true to our schizophrenic nature, the ape-person picked up another bone and used it as a weapon. We were already waltzing with both the destructive dark side of "the force," and the constructive light side of the same creative force.

This step, like many other evolutionary steps, happened "overnight." The ape-people who were able to comprehend what was happening, quickly picked up bones, too. The ape-people who did not adapt and pick up bones to use as weapons or tools, did not make it into the "new world" which quickly came into being; it was a whole new ball game. Some played, some did not, because they could not make the leap.

Why in the world did that ape-person begin to use the bone as a means to an end, rather than perceiving it in the way he always had before, as a mere bone? Because a new frequency of thought/feeling/being, was beginning to vibrate, both within the consciousness of the planet, and within the ape-person's head.

This new vibration enabled the ape-person to think/feel/be, in a more conceptual, abstract way. No longer was a bone just a bone. It could be a concept ("a weapon," and "a tool"), and it could be perceived abstractly: "If my enemy comes at some future time, I could clobber him with this bone."

The mind began to traverse time itself, if only in thought.

As the Year 2000 approaches, we face the next step on the evolutionary ladder. There is once again a new vibration in the consciousness of the planet, and within our own heads. It has to do with how we think, feel, and act as a species. It has to do with who and what we are.

My spirit guide Tibus refers to this wondrous evolutionary phase as the Healing Millennium.

It is a time of healing when we as a human race will cure ourselves of our schizophrenia and begin thinking, feeling, and being as our Whole Selves. In doing so, we will become higher beings.

It is a time of healing when we finally learn that we need not think, feel, or act with the right brain alone, or the left brain alone; thus we will no longer take two steps forward and three steps backward in our confusion, either as a human race or as individuals.

It is a time of healing when we will realize that sometimes we dance to the light side of the creative force, and sometimes we dance to the music of the dark side.

At this point in our history, we will learn to realize what is happening to us and what we are really doing when we choose to think, feel or act, to the tune of one song (dark), or the other song (light).

Just like the puppy who allows you help him, we will begin to understand what is really happening rather than blindly stumbling our way through history and through the universe, as strays.

The veil will be lifted, and we ourselves must and will do the lifting!

This evolutionary process is being activated as we speak. It is time for this to happen; the cosmic creative process dictates this, there is no stopping it.

This is what is happening right now to the consciousness of the planet and to our personal consciousness as well. This explains why things are so crazy these days.

Up until this intersect point in Space/Time, science felt it should treat cancer with radiation and harsh drugs. Spirituality felt it should treat cancer with prayer, healing colors and visualizations.

We all know people who have been helped by the scientific approach, and those who have died regardless of medical science's attempts to help, or perhaps even because of medical science's efforts to help.

We also know people who have been cured through spiritual, herbal

22

and holistic techniques, and those who have died, despite these noble efforts.

Obviously, if we combine the two, the patient would seem to have the best chance. Science keeps researching new methods of treating cancer which are less damaging to the individual, and we humans keep delving further into the spiritual cosmos as well. It would seem that the best of both worlds lies in the future and that, dancing to the music of the light side, we will one day soon, overcome the evil of cancer entirely.

Before us in the Healing Millennium, lies a time of healing when the sum of our efforts will snowball into something greater than we can imagine. When the bridge between our right and left brain is activated (and it is being activated even now), we will be a brand new species, capable of more than we ever dreamed.

This is the step on the evolutionary ladder of which we speak, this is the lifting of the veil!

CHAPTER FOUR:
THE SEVEN RAYS OF CONSCIOUSNESS

We have been referring to "the consciousness of the planet and of the individual." What composes this concoction of consciousness? Seven frequencies compose the consciousness of the human race. These seven wavelengths, or seven vibrations, compose humankind's mental and spiritual energies. They make us who and what we are.

What makes a wolf, a wolf? This creature thinks, feels, and acts as only a wolf can. It cannot be any other way; a wolf has "wolf consciousness."

Human "hum", Wolf "hum"

Artist: Pat A. Davey

In the same way, there is human consciousness which is a "hum" designating, "human." It is fascinating to study the composition of the frequency (the consciousness) of each species, but humankind is the species which is pivotal to the entire planet's salvation or destruction, and so we must concentrate on humankind.

With the coming Healing Millennium, each of the seven frequencies within the human consciousness will be raised an octave. This is a given; it **will** happen, as certainly as dawn will come at the end of night.

We can also call these seven frequencies within the human hum, The

Seven Rays. We wish to capitalize this "Seven Ray" concept, just as we have been capitalizing "Whole Self," because this concept is revolutionary and earth changing.

Long ago, the human race began capitalizing "God." Perhaps it is time that several other tremendously important concepts were capitalized.

Also, for the sake of clarity, we will refer to "Man" as we list the Seven Rays, rather than the more cumbersome, but more accurate term of "humankind." The term "Man" could also more accurately be "Man/Woman."

THE SEVEN RAYS OF HUMAN CONSCIOUSNESS

The First Ray: Man's way of thinking, feeling, and acting toward the living entity which is his mother planet.

The Second Ray: Man's way of thinking, feeling, and acting toward society, toward the tribe (or family), and toward other individuals of his species.

The Third Ray: Man's way of thinking, feeling, and acting toward the life forms who share the world with him but are not of his species. This includes plants and animals, and also the more abstract beings such as nature spirits, ghosts, angels, and other dimensional beings.

The Fourth Ray: Man's way of thinking, feeling, and acting toward his own spirituality throughout time and space. Does he have a soul? Will he be "saved?" Has he lived other lifetimes? Is he a new soul? Has he had experiences on different worlds or in different dimensions? Does his soul have a role in the distant future?

The Fifth Ray: Man's way of thinking, feeling, and acting toward all that he has yet to know and learn (The Great Unknown), including all that is "out there" in the galaxy and universe. Does Man dare to consider the possibility of alien life?

This overlaps with The Third Ray in some ways, but Ray Number Three is more specific in nature, while "The Great Unknown" is a force in itself to which Man reacts in various ways.

The nature of these reactions make a huge difference in the frequency of the species. A reaction of fear of The Unknown leads quickly to a low frequency of perception.

The Sixth Ray: Man's way of thinking, feeling and acting toward his physical body and his mental development.

The Seventh Ray: Man's way of thinking, feeling, and interacting with his Creator. He may perceive The Creator to be God, to be a number of god/goddess spirits, or to be a mindless scientific force. Regardless, Man must somehow connect to the creative source, there is a "homing device" within him to do so.

This may seem like a lot of words, a cosmic textbook list which is difficult to apply to real life.

But, The Seven Rays are the crux of real life and the key to finding your way up to the new dimension which is about to dawn. They are the texture of the consciousness of every man, woman and child; they define how each individual lives and who each individual is.

CHAPTER FIVE:
THE KEY TO THE FIRST RAY

How do you act toward your mother? With few exceptions, we love our mothers, though we realize as we grow older that mothers are "only human" and not as perfect as they seemed when we were three years old. But that image and memory of "Mother," is one which is very dear to almost everyone. Every individual on the face of the planet has a personal, genetic mother.

But what about our mother world? How do we act toward her? Most of the organized, widely accepted religions do not even recognize the "mother world" as a force within our lives.

Do you have a very early childhood memory of playing in nature on a summer day? Do you remember patting a furry little animal? And, do you accept that you, as a human being, are one of Earth's more highly evolved animals? (Perhaps you feel humans are the most highly evolved animal).

Even organized, dominant religions state that humankind has domain over the animals and forests. At least a link between humankind and nature, is acknowledged.

How has humanity treated nature? Have we treated our mother planet with gentleness and concern? She is, after all, our mother just as much as our personal, genetic mother is "Mother."

You would not have life itself if it were not for Earth, your mother planet. Do you live on Mercury? Could you survive on Jupiter? Did Pluto give you life? No, Mother Earth did.

Humankind has maintained a dismally low frequency for thousands of years where The First Ray is concerned. Remember, the First Ray: Man's way of thinking, feeling, and acting toward the living entity which is his mother planet.

In ancient times, certain tribes felt that every river had a living, breathing spirit who dwelled within the river. One could communicate with this river spirit. One could try to please her (most river spirits were considered to be female, but not all). One could ask the river spirit to treat the tribe's fishing party with care, and give many fish to the tribe. One could beg the river spirit not to let the river overflow its banks.

Ancient people would not think of polluting their helpmate, the river, which they depended on for water, food, transportation, and for spiritual inspiration.

The last two thousand years have been hard on river spirits. The belief has become instilled within humanity that God is a male persona who is "up there somewhere." This man-God apparently created the river and its spirit, but cares little about them. (How can a male force be the only entity involved in creation? How can a female force not be vitally involved, too?)

Nothing is written in The Bible about the sin of polluting the river, so chemical wastes and other pollutants have been poured into virtually every river on Earth by Man. Nothing is written about the sin of re-routing the river, destroying its ecosystem, so barges belonging to large corporations now traverse sterile, straight rivers. And if you are caught talking to "the river spirit," organized religion may well have you exorcised. A few short years ago, they might have burned you at the stake.

Little by little, humankind has been trained away from relating

27

lovingly to this planet who is a living being. Even more tragically, humankind has been trained to ignore the fact that this powerful being who gave him life, even exists.

How many worlds have created as many life forms as Mother Earth? The answer to that is, we do not know at this time. Psychically, many people feel connected to far distant planets. And, science is finding more and more worlds which might support life, as the Hubble and other modern telescopes scan the skies. But, none of us knows for sure at this point, how many planets out there, have advanced forms of life.

What we do know is that Mother Earth is a wondrous mother. She has millions of forms of life which are advanced beyond one cell organisms. They are delightful, diverse beyond imagination, adaptive, awe-inspiring forms of life. Mother Earth gives life, abundantly and splendidly.

Organized religion feels comfortable to teach us that God created life on Earth. Earth herself was a nothing-place, which had to wait for a wave of God's hand from on high.

The God Force does indeed sweep across Earth in a magnificent fashion; but, isn't The God Force another name for the living spirit of the planet? As the Healing Millennium approaches, humankind will once again begin to perceive this.

This God Force is instilled into each life which is born on Mother Earth, whether the form this life takes is human, feline, insect, or one of the myriad of other species. It is the Mother World who gives this spark, this force.

Of course, this God Force, which is also called The Creator Spirit, is afoot throughout the universe. Certainly huge forces exploded into The Big Bang and subsequently shaped the galaxies. But that precious spark which is life as it manifests in a warm kitten or an energetic two year old human, belongs at this point, to Earth alone. Do we know with certainty that any other world in the universe has bestowed life such as this?

Isn't it time, then, that humankind includes The Mother when it pays homage to its Creator?

In the past, we felt that we were "blasphemous pagans" to relate to the Mother Planet as a living entity unto herself. Organized religion demanded that we believed exactly as they taught. Fortunately, this "requirement" to give all credit to the "male God who is out there somewhere," is fast becoming outdated. No one wants to diminish God's power; we seek instead to add to our understanding of it, to enlarge our vista of our Earth Mother/Sky Father. We seek to raise our frequency. We enlighten ourselves.

As the Healing Millennium approaches, Gaia, which is the name of the living spirit of the Earth, is rising to the surface of our mass consciousness. Suddenly, we are realizing that Earth must be cherished and protected; we are now perceiving a living entity with physical and spiritual aspects. In the closing days of the old millennium, we embrace our Mother Planet, and look with joy to a more enlightened, intelligent future.

Forests must not be cut, just so that the corporate lumber industry can make more huge sums of money. Forests are the lungs of Gaia!

As the Healing Millennium approaches, Earth's living oceans must no longer be contaminated with humanity's chemical wastes. The human race will grow into maturity and realize it is wrong to kill the manatees and whales with the filth left over from our industries. Humankind has been a thoughtless adolescent until now.

The cosmos now decrees that humankind's time of thoughtless, careless adolescence, is over. We as humans cannot say, "Wait a minute, Cosmos, can't we just have another thousand years to grow up? Can't we just lay waste to our Mother Planet for a few more hundred years?"

The cosmos, and perhaps The Creator Spirit Him/Herself thunders back to us, "No! The wheel is turning, the change is coming! Grow up, Human, or die! The Healing Millennium for this beautiful Mother Planet is at hand!"

To conclude our look at The First Ray: The old frequency of consciousness regarding our living planet has been a miserable one. The Mother Planet has not even been recognized as a real life force for several thousand years.

She was viewed as something which was waved into being at the male God's whim, and it was considered "smart" to rape her forests, pollute her waters, and use up her resources in order to make as much money as possible.

That was the old, low frequency of consciousness.

The key to surviving and flourishing in the coming millennium is to allow the light to shine into your soul on this subject of your mother planet. Learn to communicate with her, love her, take care of her, and for goodness sake, at least acknowledge that she is a real and living force!

Once you have done this, work actively to save her, because she is badly damaged by the human race. Human beings have managed to nearly destroy the world on which they stand and which gave them life; it is indeed time to leave mindless adolescence and become an intelligent adult race.

Be active in environmental causes, help stray and abused animals, endangered species, do whatever you can to show your concern for Earth's many life forms and for Earth herself.

Talk to your Mother Planet when you walk in her beautiful forests, deserts, or mountains; she will answer. Learn about totems and other symbolic messages which Mother Nature sends you. Learn about her creatures, her incredible plants and trees, work with them on a spiritual level as well as being an activist for the environment.

Your concern and love will make more difference than you can possibly realize; if the human consciousness can be raised, many of the urgent crisis across the planet will begin to heal. The reality (dimension) which is "the state of the planet," will be vastly improved as the consciousness is raised; the two go hand in hand.

Miracles do happen, and they grow from perceptions within and from, the mass consciousness.

If you do succeed in raising the level of your consciousness regarding your Mother World, The First Ray in its most radiant light is yours and is a ticket into the Healing Millennium. The molecules of the Healing Millennium are composed of a risen frequency of consciousness; higher awareness makes, literally, a world of difference.

If you continue to abuse other life forms and if you fail to acknowledge the living entity which is your Mother, you will not survive in the risen frequency which is a few short years away.

The wheels of God's mind will have turned into a bright new day, away from the dark days, and you will not have "turned" with the wheel.

Remember, the turning wheel evolves into a brand new dimension. Those who do not evolve with it will become "ghosts" who ramble in the remaining threads of the old, dark dimension which has unraveled itself. This may sound a bit dramatic, but is essentially accurate. The old frequency will become extinct and those in it will become extinct also.

We have given you, then, the key to The First Ray.

CHAPTER SIX:
THE KEY TO THE SECOND RAY

The Second Ray is composed of how you think, feel, and act toward your society, your tribe, your family, and toward individuals.

It is quite clear that acting cruelly toward your family, or being insensitive to them, is a low frequency of being. Having no empathy for those you call friends and acting in your own self interest is unenlightened; soon you will have no friends, no family, if this is the way you function.

We know that blatant prejudice is wrong and is of a low level of awareness. Racial, gender, national, and religious prejudices all belong to the dark millennium from which we are emerging.

The wars of the last thousand years usually grew out of some sort of prejudice which manifested physically and devoured millions of people, with terrible deaths and untold suffering as a result.

And what is the raised frequency of The Second Ray? How can we explain The Second Ray in its most radiant light so that the second admission ticket into the dimension of the Healing Millennium is yours? The answer is simple:

Do unto others as you would have them do unto you.

Have we as a human race followed this wisdom, this high frequency of being, for the last thousand years? No, our record is absolutely miserable.

Sadly, it is the way of the late 20th Century to "get the other guy before he gets you." This seems to hold true on the freeway, in business, in relationships, and in all the other aspects of modern life. Most people do want to be honest and good, but "survival measures" seem to dictate otherwise.

A certain group of people have proved to me that the Healing Millennium will indeed be a better society where an individual can "afford" to be honest and good. Those who subscribe to my monthly newsletter, **The Star Network Heartline** and our four times a year publication, **The Change Times Quarterly**, are enlightened, loving people with whom it is a pleasure to do business, and to be friends.

These are star people, who are already of the risen frequency of consciousness. Whenever I grow pessimistic about the future of humanity, I touch bases emotionally and psychically with our many enlightened star friends, and I then know, beyond a shadow of a doubt, that the new dimension will be a beautiful one. It will be their **home** dimension; the wheels of the mind of God are returning home, slowly but surely. There is no stopping it even if we wanted to!

In the Healing Millennium the old way of mistreating others will be an extinct form of behavior; however, those who know how to love, how to give, and how to be decently honest with fellow human beings, will have no trouble adjusting to the higher frequency which emerges as the old millennium turns into the new dawn.

How wonderful, how miraculous, if we can say after the next one thousand years, that we as a human race have finally followed the path of honest, decent, positive, love. This is the simple wisdom which is the key to The Second Ray.

CHAPTER SEVEN:
THE KEY TO THE THIRD RAY

The vibration of the Third Ray is Man's way of thinking, feeling, and acting toward life forms who share this world with him but are not of his species.

In the last one thousand years, how have we treated the animals and plants who share this world?

Look at the long list of endangered animal species. Look at what has become of the once plentiful rain forests. Knock on the door of a laboratory which uses animals in cruel, and often needless experimentation. Walk along a seashore after a huge oil spill and try to clean the dying birds. There, you have your answer.

What has been our attitude as a human race, toward ghosts, fairies, gnomes, angels, demons? Have we sought enlightenment on the nature of these beings, have we treasured knowledge regarding them? Have we welcomed explorations on who or what they are?

Or have we superstitiously run scared from acknowledging that they even exist? And when we have acknowledged their existence, we have been busy burning someone at the stake who is, in our ignorant opinion, possessed by these beings.

Why is our opinion as a human race so ignorant on these subjects? It is a vicious circle of ignorance; we are ignorant because we have hidden our heads in the sand regarding these other beings. Is it any wonder that the last thousand years will be remembered as The Dark Millennium?

Our planet is overflowing with diverse forms of life; these, in the form of plants and animals, exist in the daily dimension, but many diverse life

Diane and her companion, Sinsee, on her Iowa farm

forms also exist in the other dimensions which also compose "Earth."

Our dimension is not the only one or even the dominant one. Many layers of reality share this magnificent blue/green planet with us, and each layer teems with life.

For instance, when I lived in Ireland, I began channeling a group of beings who call themselves, "The Tuatha De Danann." Originally, they were an early tribe on the island of Ireland who were said to have come from the sky.

Legend has it that they turned "sideways to the sun" (they sought another dimension of reality), when they could no longer stand the greed and cruelty of Man.

I have received transmissions from The Tuatha De Danann, which is "The Family of Diane," when translated from Irish Gaelic to English, from time to time throughout the years. They are involved in helping Earth survive the end of these dark times, and evolve onto the next higher step of reality.

In the next section of this book, we will have transmissions from one of The Tuatha De Danann and from a variety of "other dimensional" life forms, including nature spirits, fairies, astral entities, and angels. All of these life forms (sometimes we call them "light forms"), are extremely concerned that you as an individual can survive the end of the old dark days, and come with us into the Healing Millennium.

Of one thing we are sure: In the next thousand years, humankind will learn to communicate, to understand, to appreciate, and to cherish, life forms from a myriad of other dimensions who share Earth with us.

The key to The Third Ray is to be open and receptive to these other dimensional life forms, as long as they are of good intent. Very few are of totally negative intent. Humankind has been taught wrongly by The Church which desperately wanted its own authority to be absolute over humanity.

You cannot be "possessed" by the few totally negative other dimensional beings out of the blue. This is a "boogie man" which, again, has been introduced by organized religion so that you will fear knowing about the other dimensions.

You must judge other dimensional life forms the same as you judge life forms within your dimension. If you do not like them, then have nothing to do with them! If they display negative behavior or attempt to "con" you, then walk away. It is that simple. Do not fall for short cuts or for schemes which are unfair to others, or to yourself.

In The Healing Millennium, many entities, many life forms, will manifest who have not "come out of the woodwork" during the last thousand years. Be prepared for this. Be prepared to meet new life forms of which you have only dreamed. And perhaps some of which you have not even dreamed. Welcome all who are of good intent, with an open and curious attitude, in which your own good intent shines through.

This is the key to The Third Ray.

CHAPTER EIGHT:
THE KEY TO THE FOURTH RAY

The vibration of The Fourth Ray is Man's way of thinking, feeling, and acting toward his own spirituality.

For the last dark millennium, we have heard a lot about "saving our souls." But we weren't told that every soul has a rich history, both on this planet and perhaps on other worlds.

We weren't told that some of us have ancient souls while others of us have newer souls, which have just swirled out of the firmament which is Creation.

We weren't told that many souls have experienced living in the other dimensions of Earth, such as the fairy or elfin kingdoms. This is too bad because, often, an individual could understand himself better if he consciously knew of his connection to other realms. Is this why he has always felt "different?" He deserves to know of his soul's experiences so he can include those in trying to understand and value himself.

We weren't told that our souls have a part to play in the future consciousness of Earth, and perhaps, in the future of the galaxy and universe. Every soul has a cosmic history, experience, and future.

If you are ignorant as to the depth and experience of your soul, then your Fourth Ray vibration is not a high one. If you fail to recognize that other people also have this soulful history, experience, and future, you may well find yourself unable to handle the high vibration of the Healing Millennium.

But, it is more than simply knowledge regarding the soul and spirituality. It is what comes from within in terms of emotion and empathy. You must feel this!

Sometimes, an individual has not been exposed to the spiritual concepts we have just discussed. She may have been taught only that the soul needs to be saved and that the soul must believe in one narrow teaching. However, if she is a loving, empathetic soul, her vibration is a high one and she will go forward into the light of the next one thousand years.

Traditional Christianity teaches that people are lost who do not "believe," no matter how intelligent and enlightened they are; it teaches that the individual is lost even if they devoutly follow another chosen, ancient path, such as (for example), Buddhism.

It will be manifested in The Healing Millennium that all faiths and individuals become tolerant and enlightened, each for one another. No more finger pointing, no more "I have the only right religion, you do not, so you are damned to hell."

The key to the Fourth Ray is being in touch with the soul which is the God Spark within. Feel the spirit! Allow others to feel it also, in whatever way they choose.

After we explore the keys to the remaining three rays, we will have in depth channelings which include The Fourth Ray and how it shines into the Healing Millennium.

CHAPTER NINE:
THE KEY TO THE FIFTH RAY

The Fifth Ray is especially important as the new millennium approaches. For the first time in human history, we will come face to face with "people" from far distant planets which circle far distant suns.

Throughout our history, individuals have encountered extra-terrestrials and their craft, but it has always been on an individual basis when few, if any, other people were around.

We humans were not ready to meet "them" on a mass basis, they realized this. Now, the moment is coming soon. We are more ready than we were, but it is more than this. It is the intersect point in our history when we humans find it within ourselves to accept and embrace other intelligent beings, or perish as a race along with our planet.

It comes down to this: We will meet extraterrestrials if and only if, our risen frequency of mass human consciousness allows us to perceive them.

The most pivotal event in the early years of The Healing Millennium, will be mass meetings between humans and aliens in the light of day, both figuratively and literally. These momentous occasions signify, more than any other event, the risen human frequency of the new thousand years. We will be reaching out to perceive and meet them, just as much as they will be reaching out to us.

The enormous milestone of open contact with extraterrestrials ushers in The Healing Millennium.

How will you react? Will you run scared and hide your head? Will you organize "human vigilante" groups to kill every alien you see? Will you become a "human chauvinist" who thinks everything "human" is good, and everything "alien" is bad?

If so, the frequency of your mind will not mesh with the risen frequency of the new millennium.

Humanity must not embrace every extraterrestrial group with open arms. More than any point in our history, this milestone requires our logic and skepticism but also our tolerance and openness. We will have to follow our soul level intuition as we seek to know extraterrestrials as brothers and sisters. That is, we will seek to know them if they are beings of good intent. This is what we will have to decipher.

This ability to decipher whether an alien is a positive or negative being, will take a great deal of enlightenment on our part. Again, the next millennium absolutely demands that we be enlightened! We can't get by on ignorance and fear any longer.

In the millennium just passing away, one was better off not being enlightened. But, we are moving from the darkness to the light.

What cannot happen as we attempt to know our galactic brothers and sisters, is that we react with blind fear toward them. This emotion always leads to hatred and to negative psychic and emotional reactions.

Human beings have a bad record on this subject; always in our history, we feel fear for what and who we don't know; next, we develop hatred for that unknown.

There have been countless wars of tribe against tribe, religion against religion, East against West, North against South, nationality against nationality, and so on.

In the dark days, we were trained by the powers-that-be to remain constantly vigilant against a faceless "enemy" who was bound to be different from us. This difference was considered automatically to be inferior.

As the light of the new millennium approaches, it is our own internal need to evolve spiritually which demands that we stop reacting with blind fear and hatred toward the unknown.

However, in the near future, we will be dealing with greater diversity than we could possibly imagine in the past. The difference between human and alien will make minor racial differences among humans such as skin color or hair texture, seem like no difference at all.

Are we ready for this? We will have to react with more wisdom and tolerance than we ever have, in our long history as a race; we will be interacting, suddenly, with unimaginably different beings.

The key to the Fifth Ray is more than just getting ready to know and understand extraterrestrials. The Fifth Ray refers to something very deep within each of us: How do we react to "The Great Unknown?"

The Unknown is a nameless, faceless, shapeless "thing," by definition. Do we fear it instinctively? Do we assume it is very dark and very bad? Are we scared of the word "psychic?"

Do we always feel better with people who look just like us? Must we live in a town which we know and control? Do we wake up in the middle of the night scared to death of nothing in particular?

This is a low vibration, afraid of exploration, afraid of anything or anyone different.

A frequency of consciousness becomes stagnant if it continues to act and react this way. Fear paralyzes the soul's attempt to evolve spiritually.

Fearful, stagnant, reactionary souls will find The Healing Millennium is a time when there is so much hope, so much promise, and so much enlightenment, that there is no comfort and no place to hide, as there was in the old dark days.

It was alright to be scared of life itself in the last millennium. Often organized religion rewarded those who did not seek change or diversity, and admonished those who did explore change and diversity.

The universe is a place of both light and dark, but often in looking bravely into The Great Unknown, an individual finds God, not the boogie man. As an example, many who have followed spiritual and psychic quests which were frowned upon by others, have found immense serenity and fulfillment. It is up to the individual to explore with curiosity, then to decide for him or herself, if what or who has been discovered, is of worth. We are always free to reject that which feels negative to us. This is our right, and in exercising this right, we evolve spiritually. We learn, we develop. We become very proficient at intuitively recognizing good from evil.

In the next millennium we will learn not to be scared of everything and everyone who is unknown, but to analyze and empathize for ourselves.

We must evolve beyond being afraid of The Unknown; we must embrace our own path into the unknown future. The human race will raise the frequency from cowardice to bravery as we reach into the galaxy. This is the essence of The Fifth Ray.

CHAPTER TEN:
THE KEY TO THE SIXTH RAY

The Sixth Ray is Man's way of thinking, feeling and acting toward his physical body and mental development.

For the last decade of the old millennium, Man has been thinking, feeling, and acting in a more enlightened way toward his physical body.

If you doubt this, consider how your parents treated their physical bodies. They did not aim to mistreat themselves, but they probably smoked heavily, ate all the red, fatty meat they could, and didn't exercise.

In the past, did women know they should take calcium to avoid brittle bones in later years? Was the public educated on self examination for cancer in various areas of the body? Was the wonderful help of herbs taken seriously? Was the field of homeopathy even considered as viable?

The awakening which has taken place in recent years has been phenomenal.

Of course, there is farther to go; medical science still relies heavily on either prescribing potent drugs or resorting to surgery. But we hear in the news each day about progress in the medical field which makes the "Star Trek" version of medicine, a reality today.

Humanity's mental development is also an area which is moving forward incredibly fast. A few short years ago, children eagerly played video games which were beyond many adults' comprehension. Now those same video games are outdated, and children delve into interactive computers and virtual reality.

However, humanity has always been strong in the intellect department and good at technology. As the dark millennium closes, we are, as usual, highly advanced in technical innovations, but our spiritual frequency lags behind. It is our spirituality which needs to catch up.

There is a snowball effect too: Technology helps our mental development and then our mental development keeps inventing more technology, which adds to our mental development. Yes, we are doing just fine in the field of technology and intellect. But intellect is not true intelligence! Intelligence requires spirituality as well.

The drawback to our technical intellect is that we keep inventing weapons which destroy us, and machines which enslave us. Our mental efforts without accompanying spiritual wisdom, keep inventing societies which hold us captive instead of working for our benefit.

The frequency of the Sixth Ray must therefore be refined and honed. This is the only one of The Seven Rays which needs a different kind of approach, a different effort.

We must realize that our mental abilities must adhere to the guidance of our spiritual conscience. It is our spirituality which needs to take a huge step forward.

Spirituality must begin to take the lead in our thinking, feeling, and acting toward our physical bodies. For instance, the question "to clone or not to clone" is in the forefront as the dark millennium ends. In the next section, we will have a channeling on the subject of cloning.

There are many other similar critical subjects which we will also discuss. These subjects require that we use our integrity and our spirituality to answer questions which our technical development now puts before us.

The key to The Sixth Ray is that we must bring its frequency into harmony and balance with the frequencies of the other six rays. What is good, right, and decent, must lead the way.

Technology in itself has no conscience. Science in itself is cold and self serving. If we allow technology and science to dominate as the next millennium begins, there will be no future.

However, the future does already exist in the Healing Millennium. It is for those who awaken spiritually and learn to control technology.

Lead with the spirit. Allow science and technology to assist you if you wish, but they must never lead. This is the key to The Sixth Ray.

CHAPTER ELEVEN:
THE KEY TO THE SEVENTH RAY

The Seventh Ray is Man's way of thinking, feeling, and acting toward his Creator.

It is fitting and proper that the culmination of The Seven Rays is "The God Ray." As we raise the frequency of the other six, we sail to the risen frequency of the seventh; we arrive at the farthest point of outer space, and the closest point of inner space. We touch the face of God. God within, God without. God above. God below. God all around.

In New Age circles, God has a variety of conceptual names, and so it will be in the Healing Millennium when diversity will be embraced and celebrated, not scorned.

Buddhism gives us "The All That Is." Native Americans refer to "The Creator Spirit."

Nirvana, Godhead, Universal Law, Christ Consciousness. All of these are good attempts to word what is unwordable.

It's interesting to note that "Nirvana" refers to a state of being which the individual attains rather than a separate entity who is "God." This is helpful as we stand at the threshold of the Healing Millennium and find that God is a spark within us.

What about someone who believes there are gods and goddesses, but no monotheistic God? In the Healing Millennium, we embrace this individual and his beliefs. We find it fascinating to realize that God may be a spark within us all, while gods and goddesses may be separate, outside entities. Most of all, we know that this individual who believes in gods and goddesses will never again be ostracized and tortured for his beliefs, as he was in the old dark millennium.

This is the true measure of the risen frequency of our Seventh Ray.

In a real way, The Healing Millennium is all about coming face to face with God. We will return to the "creation stuff" from which we spun away, those thousands of years ago. Our homing device within will lead us home, to our Creator.

We may find this "creation stuff" far out in the galaxy, deep inside other dimensional Earth, or in the micro-world of the microscope.

But, we take it with us, too, because we already have it. We are God.

The God Spark within is the most holy of holies. This is the key to The Seventh Ray.

CHAPTER TWELVE:
A GUIDE TO RAISING THE FREQUENCY OF THE SEVEN RAYS

For sixteen years, I have been involved in channeling messages from various entities. The only requirement I have for allowing them to send their transmissions through me is that they be of good intent.

Sometimes I have received an angry message from an equally angry entity. An example of this are the transmissions I have received from "the spirit of the volcano" who calls herself "B'Tamei." She tells us that she is an amoral entity who wishes us neither good nor harm, but that she is the emotional vent for Mother Earth's anger at what humanity has done to her.

I have made myself available to B'Tamei because her messages have voiced concern and warning, and have also expressed hope for the future. She is not evil, she is simply a natural spirit.

Usually, the messages I receive are from spiritually evolved beings of the higher realms. Their messages include urgent advice on how to help save our dying world, and they always send renewed strength, love, and great optimism.

These light beings insist that they are with us more than we might possibly realize, in our current struggle to survive this dark intersect point in time, as we walk our path toward the New Dawn.

My star guardian Tibus sends by far the most messages to me, and is with me on a daily personal basis as well. His guidance and protection has saved me more than once from danger.

What I did not realize as I channeled the many messages throughout these fifteen years, was that each message could be connected into one of The Seven Rays. I did not consciously realize that a blueprint has been unfolding on how and why we as a human race must raise the frequency of our Seven Rays.

In other words, we as a planetary race have a way of thinking, feeling, and acting toward our mother world, toward each other, toward the life forms who share our world, and so on.

Unfortunately, our low vibration belongs to the passing dark millennium. We must now raise our vibration regarding these seven subjects (The Seven Rays), and evolve spiritually, or perish.

When I received the many transmissions I have channeled throughout fifteen years, I had no idea they would fit into this blueprint as they now do! Tibus and his friends of space and dimension, had this blueprint all along; it has all come together right now as we move into the new millennium!

Tibus and his friends assure us that the process of evolution is easier than it sounds. He reminds us that "change" can never be perceived as it happens; it is either right before, or right after "change."

Currently, we exist at a moment just before a major change of dimension, a turning of the page of reality. Before we know it, it will be "after."

Tibus also reminds us that even Earth scientists now agree that many steps in evolution for a variety of species, have happened virtually overnight. For many years, it was thought that every evolutionary process took hundreds or thousands of years.

Although an evolutionary process may be "building steam" for hundreds or thousands of years, some major steps in evolution have happened literally overnight.

An example of "overnight evolution" is when the ape-person first picked up a bone as a weapon. That took one second, though he or she may have pondered picking it up for a few seconds before actually making the move. In that one second, nothing was ever the same again. All the other ape-people had to pick up weapons or be killed by the weapon-wielder. Even if it took ten years for the concept of "pick up a weapon" to spread throughout the ape-people tribes, this huge step in evolution took a few short years.

How much closer are you to making a huge step in evolution than you were ten years ago? We confirm that you are unimaginably closer! Your spiritual explorations and experiences have allowed you to cover in a few short years what might have taken a thousand years to realize in "normal" historic times. The force of evolution is with you!

These are not normal times! Not only is the momentous millennium change approaching, which is always a traumatic time in human history, this is also the one and only "Change Times" for Planet Earth. Tibus has told us that every planet faces its Change Times sooner or later.

Humankind has done so much damage to the planet that entire ecosystems are threatened and already Mother Earth has attempted to make many adaptations to her new handicapped state.

Humans have managed to weaken the immune system of the planet; the main factor in Earth's immune system is her ozone layer. We have punched huge holes in it and made it thinner all over the globe, with our nuclear testing and our aerosol cans.

Humans have burned down the Mother Planet's rain forests in order to have huge herds of cows graze, in order to kill them, in order to eat very cheap, padded hamburgers. No, these are not normal times!

The list of crisis is endless at this point in time, on this planet. In our book **Earth Changes Bible**, we deal with the many specific, urgent problems and how we might overcome them. Now, in this book, we offer an even more specific blueprint for turning the page on this dark moment in history, and for ushering in a better world, a planet which has healed.

The Healing Millennium affords us this miraculous opportunity with its own inherent cosmic energies. It is our last chance.

You see, we not only perceive our reality, we participate in it. Our problems as a planet are so far reaching and serious that the only answer is to turn the page of reality. We need to create a completely new dimension. How wonderful that the energies which are about to dawn will assist us in doing this; this is the promise of The Healing Millennium. With the help of these cosmic energies, we can do it!

How exactly can we do this? With our minds and souls. We do it with our perception and participation in reality. We do it by using this blueprint which gives these ancient, mystical, Seven Rays of Consciousness. These are our spirit, our being.

We must raise the frequency of these rays within ourselves. If you wish, you may symbolize this as intensifying the color of these rays, from drab blue to deep indigo blue. From pale green to living, lush, forest green. From cream color to sunbright yellow. From sickly orange to brilliant sunset orange. From light pink to hot rose pink. From watered red to radiant, flaming red. From weak lavender to vibrant, dynamic purple.

Or, you may wish to symbolize them as notes of an octave coming into full harmonic beauty after years of broken chords and wrong notes.

In upcoming chapters, you will hear from a chorus of universal beings. Each has a transmission for us which will fit into our master blueprint.

Some give detailed information on obtaining our new, higher frequency within the rainbow of The Seven Rays Of Conscousness.

Other transmissions outline a number of urgent global crisis and tell us how to act on them spiritually and psychically. These are extremely important because our spiritual and psychic power can transform these doomsday crisis into a new and better dimension which has a bright future!

How can we on Earth do this? Our universal friends of Space/Time, will tell us, precisely and clearly.

CHAPTER THIRTEEN:
TO CLONE OR NOT TO CLONE

This is Tibus. I come to you in love and light.

Cloning: Of course, they have already cloned a human being, does anyone doubt this? We must give the severe warning: Humankind is not ready spiritually and morally, to possess this ability!

Technically, humankind has now found the key to cloning, which is not difficult as technology goes. This key was found years ago, and has been used to clone humans already.

The fact that it was recently that a sheep was successfully cloned, indicates that it was feared the "cloning reality" would be exposed to the masses soon; it was decided that the public should be told about "Dolly the Cloned Sheep." Thus, discussions were initiated on the many bizarre doors cloning opens, while admitting that the cloning of a human being could be "only a few years away."

As you know, cloning raises enormous moral, spiritual issues. Does a wealthy man keep a clone of himself handy for organ replacement should it become necessary?

Is that clone an individual with human rights?

Does that clone have a soul? Does that clone live a normal life of wear and tear or is he kept in stasis, since his "purpose" is to give fresh organs to the wealthy man?

And of course, a wealthy man would not feel secure with one clone, why not have ten to make sure there is always an organ available! Do those ten clones owe their lives to "their creator," the wealthy man? But isn't each one of them really him?

Perhaps one of clones would stage a coup and replace the wealthy man, making him a "clone" for the new "original." Then, the original wealthy man can sit in stasis and wait to give the new "top dog" an organ or two.

On the other hand, are all clones and their "original" so totally equal to each other (since they are each other), that total stagnation sets in, with no dominant?

Perhaps the clones would be stronger because they would have lived perfect lives, whereas the original wealthy man smoked, ate too much, had several accidents, suffered from stress, and in general diminished his health and fitness over the years.

Someone might say to you, "None of these scenarios will come about because we plan to clone only parts of individuals." It was reported recently that scientists want to clone human torsos, organs, even brain stems, without allowing the clone's brain to complete itself. Do these scientists really believe that science will stop short of completed clones? Do we really think humankind is so decent as to stop before going "all the way" with clones?

Once there is just one completed clone, there will be others. In fact, this has already happened; the cat is already out of the proverbial bag. So, promises of growing partial clones are already broken. And for that matter, who is to say that a "partial clone" does not have feelings and cannot be hurt? Yes, they say they will not grow the clone's central nervous system. And I have a bridge in Brooklyn to sell you.

Or let us consider a more sympathetic scenario with a clone: The only child of loving, wealthy parents, develops a fatal disease. The parents try everything to save the child but finally decide to clone their offspring before the original dies. Do parents of middle and lower socio-economic classes also have this option? Cloning will take a lot of money for the foreseeable future. Will there even be room for the middle and lower socio-economic classes with the wealthy cloning themselves to their content?

Another question: Does the "replacement" child somehow diminish the life and passing of the original? Will anyone really notice or care when the original does pass on, as they cluster around the clone?

Does this scenario go against the bigger cosmic picture wherein souls sometimes stay with a family for a few years but wish to go onward, not staying for an entire lifetime? Often there is a beautiful reason why they stay with a family for a few years, then choose to go onward for other equally noble, good reasons.

Does the replacement child have a soul?

Is it the same soul as the original? How can it be, when the original child has a cosmic path to follow, from lifetime to lifetime?

Might the clone hold the original's soul to Earth when the higher plan was for the original to travel onward? Will the "dead" original enter a terrible limbo state because the soul has entered the clone?

Even if "soul" is a bit of a subjective term for you of scientific persuasion, you will admit that each individual is composed of three aspects: Her genetics (heredity), her environmental experiences, and her unique individual "stuff" (personality).

It is this unique personality of which I speak. This is the spiritual aspect of every individual. We call it, The God link. We call it, the soul.

Allow me to give you a specific scenario which raises yet another moral and spiritual question regarding cloning: Consider the murder of the little daughter of wealthy people. Would anyone know she had been murdered if a clone had already been made? How many little girls (clones of the original) would be sexually molested, abused, and murdered as time went along? And what of her baby sister? A scenario like this creates a new level of horror such as the human race has not yet experienced.

The number of specific scenarios is endless and mind boggling, and yet for all of these, you cannot begin to imagine the enormity and complexity of the horrific possibilities.

Human life is cheap enough on city streets and elsewhere. How cheap will it become when clones are readily available; no will be sure who is "clone" and who is "original," and why care anyway? The financially poor will not be replaced, but the wealthy will go on endlessly. And, should the financially impoverished gain the right to clone, with the government paying for it, does this help anything?

Let me answer several nagging questions: Do clones have souls?

Might clones be mindless madmen?

Might clones "rob" the original of his soul after he passes on?

Might the soul of the "dead" man sail into the clone, thus making a soulless zombie of the original who passed on?

In answer to the first question, "Do clones have souls?" Usually clones are docile and "mediocre." There is not that wild, wonderful flame of life which originals have. The Creator did not directly breathe the magnificent spark of life into the clone. This reality in itself tends to make "originals" treat clones as inferiors, it creates an almost automatic subclass.
However, it would be wrong to feel that clones do not have souls; they do.

Clones are valid life forms, and the tendency to devalue them is wrong; in a basic sense, The Creator did create them, in a roundabout way. It would seem they have the hereditary and environmental aspects, but the elusive "soul" has a quieter voice. It may well be that the soul of a clone is simply not experienced, not ancient, but rather is a fresh bit of God Spark.

Unfortunately, humankind hasn't overcome his tendency to feel other "races" within the human race to be inferior, so how can he possibly attain the fine sensibility, decency, and sensitivity to be fair to clones? Humankind is not spiritually ready for the issues raised by cloning!

To answer the second question, occasionally a clone is something of a mindless madman. Usually, this does not happen. It seems that in finding souls for clones amongst the fresh God Spark "stuff," occasionally nothing good can be found, and something negative enters.

The clone's existence summons "energies" just as a ouija board summons "energies." There is a vacuum, so to speak, which cosmic energy must fill. There is a chance that a totally negative energy will enter as "the soul."

In answer to the third question, clones do not chain to Earth, the soul of the original who has passed on. The original soul goes its own way, invariably. But this does leave an empty vacuum which will be filled one way or another. The clone might have every similarity to the original (even seemingly the same personality), but the "fire within" and the source of motivation, will be different from the original.

The unique "fire within" belongs to the original alone. And the unique fire which the clone has, belongs uniquely to him. Is he not, then, a completed human who has a right to live his own life, and not to serve as an organ replacement mannequin for an original?

Clones are usually created for a specific purpose which another individual has pre-planned, even if it is not as an organ replacement specimen. Whatever the purpose, no individual has the right to impose this on another. Each individual has the right to find his or her own purpose in life.

How do I, Tibus, know all this, you might ask? Because my voice is from the future; that is, the future of the human race. The Seven Rays of my being are attuned to the frequency of the Future Human Consciousness.

In my time and reality, we have dealt with the challenge of cloning; we have argued the issues. Subsequently, we have made rules which must not be broken.

We survived the "age of cloning" but we learned many hard, hurtful lessons. We do not clone anymore. At best, it was a miserable failure, shaking our morality and spirituality to its core.

Why don't I simply let you at this point in time, find out the hard way? My colleagues and I are, in fact, not physically interfering with your experimentation. We would not do this.

However, it is our obligation as your "big brothers and sisters," to give you our heartfelt advice and to beg you as passionately as we can, to stop the "craft" of cloning before it gets a firm foothold in your society!

You might ask, "If you of the future survived your time of cloning, then don't we automatically survive it (since "you" are "us")? Therefore, why worry? Let's have fun and experiment. We'll learn our lesson as we are supposed to."

In **Earth Changes Bible**, we explained in detail, the concept of "The Reality Continuum." It is our humble attempt to tell you that there are a number of alternate realities. You as a human race, will follow one of them. The human race from another reality, will follow another outcome.

All possibilities exist for you at this moment, both as an individual and as a member of the human race. The future is not written in stone; you create it as you go along, my friend.

We urge you to read **Earth Changes Bible** for more information on alternate realities, and on The Reality Continuum.

Regarding cloning, suffice it to say that in some human futures, cloning spells the end of the vigor of the race and the loss of morals and traditions of human society. All enlightenment is lost which humankind had struggled to establish for thousands of years. Cloning contributes greatly to this future nightmare reality, with heart wrenching problems which the best of science fiction writers cannot begin to imagine.

In other human futures, cloning is abandoned. The inherent problems and evils involved in it, are perceived clearly, and the human race responds with decency and decisiveness. This is why I give you the benefit of our wisdom; do all you can to make your future reality, a positive one.

There are many shades of realities in the future branches which you humans will create. Some alternate realities are absolutely beautiful, others are absolutely horrible. And, doomsday for the human race and the entire planet, awaits as the worst possible future. Which will it be? The decisions which you make today, will determine this. The spiritual and psychic power you put into force today, determines the future.

You might ask if there are races who employ the practice of cloning. There are races in the galaxy and in the universe who employ this practice.

Reports of abductions of human beings by negative (grey) aliens who are similar, mechanized, and lacking in decency, indicate that this group is indeed a group of clones. In fact, we have not yet encountered a race which clones which has great vigor or great passion for being of good intent.

I point out here that cloning can be a "necessity" when a race becomes sterile due to having abused nuclear or other powerful energies. However, the evil of the abuse of nuclear power continues to haunt the race which abused it, because their efforts to clone themselves, do not create a vigrous and decent "new" race. All beings need that direct "breath of God" to be breathed into them.

I state that no member of our Space/Dimensional Intelligence practices cloning. Sometimes we just call ourselves "the good guys."

Incidentally, it is always your choice and responsibility to decide which of us is good and which is evil. Judge us by our actions. Ultimately, look into your own heart and soul; look to your own guidance. But, please don't make the mistake of feeling we are all "bad" simply because we are from "The Great Unknown."

You may agree with all I have pointed out regarding the craft of cloning, but you might be wondering, how can you stop your government or private researchers, from continuing on the cloning path?

You cannot physically march on their laboratories, this is true. You can of course oppose cloning politically and ethically, this cannot hurt. Sadly, governments and private researchers do not listen to "the people" anymore.

The simple and only answer is: You must turn the page! Create a new dimension. You as a part of the mass human consciousness can do it. We have given you the seven mystical components of your human consciousness to help you perceive all which is required of you.

Remember, the wondrous news: The mass human consciousness is indeed rising in frequency as The Healing Millennium becomes reality! The cosmic wheel, which is the Mind of God, is turning toward a new phase. The dark days are being left behind, the light will shine, regardless.

You have only to aim the vibration of your consciousness at this new, brighter day.

You might think I am contradicting myself: Should you work to help raise the frequency? Or is the frequency going to raise itself, anyway? It is indeed difficult to word that which is unwordable, but I shall try:

The train will indeed leave the station. This "train" is actually the rising vibration of human consciousness. It is indeed evolving.

If you get on this train, you will arrive in The Healing Millennium. The year 2001 is the future, and has great hope and promise. The train is going into the daylight, leaving the darkness.

However, if you stand at the station and do not bother to get on the train, you will stand in darkness. The train will leave without you.

This darkness will fade out and become "nothingness" soon, like the curtain lowering on a play.

To understand this, consider the concept of "the past." It is over, and is now "nothing." You cannot interact with it anymore. You can only remember it and whatever lessons you might have learned there.

The train does exist. This is another way of saying, The Healing Millennium does exist. The mind of God is turning without fail, toward a bright new day, away from the darkness of the past thousand years.

You will create the fact that you walk toward the train and step onto it. You create your own higher awareness through your cosmic explorations and experiences. You allow your mind and soul to open to the light. You and the train intersect, and head toward the future.

To return for a moment to the subject of cloning: When the frequency is raised, a world will exist in which cloning researchers no longer exist. No funds from supportive governments or organizations will be given to further the research. The level of consciousness will mandate that cloning experimentation does not take place.

In fact, such governments and organizations will find themselves extinct also. Enlightened people will have concluded that they are not needed for "control," and that they do more harm than good. They will not find an atmosphere in which they can exist. No one will support them.

If individuals who compose these groups and organizations cannot manage to "get on the train," they will be left in darkness. We of Space/Time Intelligence do not decree this; it is the individual human who makes this choice for him or herself. The cosmic wheel turns, none of us can stop it. A tidal wave of light is about to sweep through the consciousness of the human race.

Evolution is pure magic. Evolution is a miracle. It can and does happen overnight. This is what is about to happen: Homo sapiens is about to become Homo cosmos. Work toward this. Prepare. The page turns, not little by little, but with one sweep of The Creator's Hand.

May the healing light of God and goodness surround you, always,
Tibus

UFO Occupant

Artist: Merrilee Miller

CHAPTER FOURTEEN:
VERITAN SPEAKS HIS MIND

This is Veritan. I come to you in the light of logic.

I have had the honor of channeling messages through Diane's consciousness on a number of occasions. In **Earth Changes Bible**, I was introduced to you as a "sometimes befuddled alien." I suppose that is an accurate description of my attempts to transmit within the human consciousness frequency. I do not aim to sound snobbish; though my race of beings is universally considered to be of higher awareness than the human race at this point (we survived our own Change Times many eons ago), it is simply that the human frequency is **different** for me.

I am a mathematician/scientist by "trade" but I am guided first and foremost by my spirit and integrity. Any form of life is sacred to me.

I cherish logic; it is a scarce and precious commodity on Earth. Humans act and react with emotion; logic is a poor second when it comes to human behavior.

I do aim to be critical. Emotion can cause humans to act very bravely; you might well jump in an icy river to save another individual even if you could not swim. Logic would dictate that you would also drown so should not jump in. By some miracle, your emotional response of jumping into the river might save the drowning person and, hopefully, you would be saved also. However, logically, you both would drown. The act of trying to save another life is very noble.

However, human emotional response has been appealed to over and over again throughout your history, to drive you to fight wars, to kill, to hate, to ostracize, to believe your way, religion, or race, are superior to others.

Who has driven you? Evil, greedy, power hungry opportunists you believe to be your leaders, your churches, or your governments.

The emotional aspects of being human should be cherished, but these must now be blended with enlightenment, intelligence, and, yes, logic. The spirit must lead, but true spirit is much more than emotionalism.

I am very pleased with my own progress in the skill of channeling. It dawns on me that I am one of the most regular contributors to our efforts in reaching enlightened human beings, whom we call "star people."

Star people do not need to have had a UFO experience or to be "special" in any unusual way. "Star people" are, simply, those humans who have obtained higher awareness. You, who are reading this book, are "the enlightened ones."

I hope you do not mind if my colleagues and I refer to you as "the star people." You are a human who has sufficient awareness to bridge from past to future, from darkness to the light. You are truly the hope (the only hope!) of the human race. Know how special you are. Treasure this frequency of consciousness at which you have arrived, and build on it.

I also always seek to build on the frequency of consciousness I have obtained. No one in the universe should be stagnant in their spiritual explorations. If they become stagnant, theirs is not a high frequency.

I have also been improving my telepathic success rate with individuals; there are those who know me as their star guardian and spirit guide. I am ready to be a spiritual friend to whomever wishes to know me. I do not feel as awkward as I did a brief time ago when dealing with humans who reflect Twentieth Century culture. Even though you are not a typical Twentieth Century individual, you still reflect that spot in Space/Time in which you dwell.

I am not of the Future Human Consciousness, I am an alien in all senses of the world to your planet. I have spent over 900 years in Earth terms, in pursuit of being a good, competent cosmic mathematician and scientist. My infancy was spent on a far distant planet and my immediate family dwells there.

I have many friends within the Space/Dimensional Intelligence for whom I "work." Space/Dimensional Intelligence is our name for the whole bunch of "good guys" working with the human race and Planet Earth in this crisis time.

I have experienced several human lifetimes but I remained a "resident alien" in vibration. You may know this feeling, too.

It would be impossible to work with the human vibration if one had no experience at all as a human being. I dare say, all of us who work with you have some kind of experience in being human at some point in time.

While helping other "resident aliens" on Earth, I also have a chance to resolve several bothersome echoes in my own vibration, because my lifetimes as a human being were not the most successful. That is, unless you would call being tortured to death in the Spanish Inquisition "successful;" this happened because I didn't know how not to be, logical!

What I want to do beyond in this transmission is to give you hints on how not to panic at what is happening. I hope to fly with you above the trees for an overview of the forest below. This technique is very important if you are to survive coming times of mass hysteria, trauma, and chaos.

Without this higher perspective, paranoia and blind fear set in, doing more harm than the worst of actual events. Fear is always the greatest enemy; we call it The Fear Factor. In the past, it has been used to control large masses of human beings, but you as an entire species are about to throw off this yoke.

Fear is always the "wild card" when working with psychic energy also. It is a human emotion you must learn to control; work above and beyond it! These are not mere words or slogans, this is truth.

The psychic abilities of the human species are held down by The Fear Factor. Either you are afraid to allow your psychic powers to fly free and they become impotent, or you mingle The Fear Factor with your psychic effort and contact negative beings.

Those individuals who have been involved with positive metaphysics for years will tell you, "Do not let fear enter when you are working with metaphysical energies. Bathe yourself with the golden light of good intent and positive feeling, and enjoy your exploration."

Now, allow me to get down to business. There is so much to be concerned about as the last years of the dark millennium melt away, and The Healing Millennium shines before us. We enlightened individuals, human and alien, have too much to attend to, too much to apply our concentration to, do we not?

As these Earth Changes leap forward, it is confusing! Which crisis should we turn our attention to next? Everything is falling apart at once.

But, this is the definition of "Change Times." This is what we all came to Earth for. Remember, Earth is not alone in going through this crisis. All worlds which give birth to life, face a time of greatest crisis when survival is in question.

Everything is indeed changing. It is enough to make me wish for my secure, predictable mathematics career on my home world. However, like you, I am totally committed to these Earth Change Times with little time for more pleasurable activities. And, I am very busy mathematically as we keep a scientific finger on the pulse of the planet.

I wish to mention a specific area of concern now. Enlightened people are acutely aware that rights and freedoms are being taken. These usually come in the form of this law or that regulation which is supposed to make society better or safer.

Society does need to be better and safer, but everyone is aware of how absurd things have become, restricting good people unfairly, encroaching on their privacy and freedom, while bad people are not really affected (by these regulations and laws). What is the definition of a "police state?" Is it not exactly what is happening?

There are many publications which attempt to tell people their version of what is happening, and most state that they love their country but do not anymore love their government. What is happening is so strange and wrong, that the terms "right" and "left" don't even apply anymore.

Read whatever publications you feel are telling the truth.

I want you to know, we of Space/Dimensional Intelligence are highly aware of this very real worldwide crisis. It is symptomatic of Earth Changes.

We do not belabor specific political subjects in our channelings. We realize that our star people are very aware and intelligent, and you think for yourself.

But we are aware, and we do delve into implications and possibilities in order to stay a step ahead. We love freedom as deeply as you do; we can only say, we know that it will be alright! You must raise the frequency in order to be rid of this plague!

Freedom to pursue life, liberty and happiness is a planetwide right and concern. It is also the given right of all beings throughout the galaxy and the universe. You are not alone!

Remember that I am endeavoring to give you knowledge and wisdom which will enable The Seven Rays of your consciousness to become even more vibrant and of high frequency. We do not dictate to you what to think or believe as others have done in the past. We instead urge you as a human race to "grow up" at this moment in time and thus think, feel, and act with greater intelligence and enlightenment.

Humanity must demand that it be told the truth. You must refuse to allow governments to lie so blatantly and horrendously to you. Governments are created only to serve you, the people. When they become self serving multi-national entities, it is time they became extinct.

We are very concerned that the human race also realizes that there is a spiritual choice which must be made at this point. It is well and good to know the truth; for instance, the majority of humans realize that UFOs are real and that their occupants are visiting Earth. But there is much more than that to these strange days!

There is for the human race, a choice to be made: Do you choose the Light Side of The Force? Or the Dark Side of The Force? It is true that without the darkness, there can be no light. No one is arguing that you should go forth and exterminate the Dark Side; then, wouldn't you be the Dark Side?

Have you not been the Dark Side for thousands of years, causing wars, famine, suffering, and death for one another and for other life forms?

Will the human race choose to meet the challenge and evolve spiritually, taking a step upward? If you do choose that step upward, you then embrace the Light Side of the Force. You choose life.

Remember, there are aliens visiting Earth who function on The Light (frequency), and there are aliens visiting here whose "hum" is definitely on the Dark Side.

By Dark Side, we do not mean black cats, bats and the misty midnight moon. We mean arrogant, mindless technology, running uncontrolled, protected by heartless, self serving bureaucracy.

We mean greedy, cold science without any morality, integrity, or empathy, which answers to no one.

We mean hatred and prejudice against those who are "different" or who don't conform. That's the Dark Side of The Force.

Empathy, compassion, spirit, nobility, vulnerability, humor, endurance, integrity, hope, sweet melancholy, charity, gentleness, serenity, joy, wonder, intelligence, the openness to love unconditionally. These are the Light Side.

A word about collusion between negative aliens and the governments and militaries of Earth: It is accurate to say that we good guys are not easily understood by Earth governments and militaries. These agencies find negative aliens much easier to understand and to work with. They share the same frequency.

However, as Gene Roddenberry, the creator of "Star Trek" said, "The people of Earth are Light Years ahead of their petty governments!" We good guys find the people of Earth much easier to work with; we simply could not "do business" with the governments and militaries.

In the same way, many of the people of Earth are too decent to do business with negative aliens. The people of Earth do not, in general, find the bad guys and their methods, appealing; this is one reason there is great hope. The awareness level of humanity is raising itself, and most people are of goodness.

Ultimately, the agencies and the bad aliens cannot win.

Humanity must perceive that what is happening at this time is not frightening, it is not "the end," but it is a wondrously positive step forward. It is not everyday that Homo sapiens becomes Homo cosmos. Humans must now seize the day, adapt, and rejoice!

You must create a new level of reality, then take that leap up to it. The old step on which humankind stood for millennia, will not hold any longer. It is crumbling, but there must not be panic.

The human soul is created to exist in balance and harmony with The Creator and the Universe. Humanity must now rise above disharmony and imbalance, and move toward cosmic citizenship.

This cosmic status is the original source of the human race, and the human race has an unalienable right to this status.

With this said, I must move on to a tragic reality: There is severe global warming on Earth; in the Antarctic, The Larsen Ice Shelf is disintegrating at an alarming rate. It is melting more quickly than anyone had imagined it would.

Do not let conspiracy "experts" tell you that global warming is just a ploy by the government to divert your attention from evil actions by the government. This story has been making the rounds recently. If you believe this, it will divert your psychic energies from this legitimate crisis. The situation of melting polar ice caps grows worse and worse.

Yes, there are plenty of ploys, much disinformation, many downright lies, in an attempt to keep the populace under control and to keep truths hidden. But, global warming and the disintegrating ice shelves are a real and severe crisis!

As a matter of fact, the truth of the severity of this situation is repressed by the mass media. This crisis should be the headline each day! It is certainly more important than the many attention diverting, highly emotional items which do compose the headlines.

You must work on creating a reality in which the melted ice shelves do not flood all land, creating terrible storms and violently altering the face of Earth. The rate of melting can be slowed through reality-creating psychic energies.

Remember all we have told you about the nature of reality (perceived and participated in), and how you can turn the entire dark page if only you will.

At the close of this book, we will give you specific information on how you can join efforts to spiritually and psychically raise the frequency, thus turning the page.

You must realize that a "melt" can indeed occur more gently and less radically. Your calm, gentle, loving energies transmitted into the Fabric of Reality will help this "gentle melt" to occur, and assist the melting process to halt. Global warming can also be slowed, then halted, in this way.

Remember our Reality Continuum with alternate realities: There are bound to be serious climate problems, but they do not have to be catastrophic, deadly results.

In a very real sense, humanity's neglect, abuse, and irreverence to its Mother Planet has caused the reality which now confronts us. Negative thought and action led to the negative reality of global warming and damaged ozone layer.

In his greed, humankind stopped holding his Mother Planet sacred; this led to the sorry state in which humanity and his planet find themselves. This reality was created by humankind. Humankind can re-create a better reality than this! It is not too late.

Reality can be manipulated; the future is not written in stone.

On the Reality Continuum, a "1" means "no change at all." Applying this to the Change Times, we can conclude that a "1" would mean there were no signs of Earth Changes at all; there would be no Change Times. Global warming, melting ice, violent storms, earthquakes, volcanoes, viruses, society breaking down, the One World Order threat, all of this would not have taken root at all. We know well that Earth has already passed up the "1," because no one can deny that there are sweeping Earth Changes taking place.

Our Reality Continuum runs to "10." Applying this to the Change Times, a "10" on the continuum is Doomsday, the end of all life on Planet Earth. If individuals sit and do nothing, this is what will occur.

Better to create an "8" on the Reality Continuum, wherein millions of lives are lost in catastrophic events, but the spark of life itself, goes on. There would still be a few human beings and many other species which survived.

But, how much better to live through a "5" on the continuum, wherein Earth does undergo huge changes in climate and society, but only thousands die, not millions or billions. For those who prepare well, Earth Changes mean hardship but not injury or death.

And if a "5" can be reached, why not nudge reality to a "4" with even less damage and death? Create it with the power of your mind.

This explanation is a bit simplistic, but I hope it conveys the concept. We of Space/Time Intelligence, readily acknowledge and embrace the fact that we can and do create our own reality. Perhaps that is why our dimension is "higher" than those beings who do not realize this crucial fact.

Envision a world wherein Earth Changes are not devastating or deadly. Envision a world which is a phoenix, risen from the ashes, a world of higher consciousness.

The longer an enlightened soul like you survives, helping to weave the fabric of reality, the longer the hope of a new and better world survives.

Consider it this way: If you, my enlightened friend, survive into that new day, then the world has survived into a new day!
Therefore, prepare well and be determined to survive.

Some of the threats to Planet Earth which humankind has brought about, also threaten other dimensions of Earth in which dwell many varieties of beings.
Some of these interdimensional beings are members of our Space/Time Intelligence; they are enlightened, wondrous life forms, and our friends. This is an added reason for us to be concerned and to offer our help to you as we are at this moment.

I have spoken long enough for now. I thank our channel Diane for patching me through to you.

Go in light, love, and logic,
Veritan

CHAPTER FIFTEEN:
TIBUS ON INNER EARTH DWELLERS

This is Tibus. I come to you in love and light.

In **Earth Changes Bible,** you will remember our predictions about "the rings of fire" becoming activated across Planet Earth in the months ahead. From Italy to Montserrat, these predictions are proving to be correct.

Volcanoes are interconnected to each other across the planet through elaborate, deep tunnels and tubes, nestled deep into Mother Earth.

Many other-dimensional beings dwell in Inner Earth and use these tunnels for transportation; they do not walk through them, because most of these beings are of a higher (lighter) density which allows them to move through what seems to be solid material to those in the three dimensional reality.

Volcanic tunnels and tubes are essential to the lives and well being of these other-dimensional beings; even now, the rapidly increasing vulcan activity is disturbing their way of life. They have told us recently that they are being driven to the surface in these last several years of the dark millennium.

I remind you, that other-dimensional beings are no different from other universal beings; some Inner Earth beings are completely of good intent, and very high frequency of consciousness, while others are not as evolved.

The universe is made up of positive and negative molecules; this is as-should-be. There is balance, a miracle of The Creator Spirit's magnificent energies.

Remember that one quadrant of the sky does not create good beings while another quadrant creates negative beings. Not all Pleiadeans are good and not all Orions are bad. These constellations cover many thousands of stars with many hundreds of planets supporting intelligent life within them.

In the same way, not everyone from Inner Earth is the creepy, negative being which stereotypically is said to dwell "in the bowels of the Earth."

In fact, a vast majority of Inner Earth dwellers are extremely intelligent, gentle, wise, beings. They are also very ancient beings, and have amassed the wisdom of the ages; wisdom which humankind often does not remember. Much can be learned from them.

One reason you personally must come to know and love Gaia, the living Spirit of Earth, is that you may well meet her Inner Dwellers in the future. You must be intelligent and advanced enough not to apply stereotypes and run the other way in utter fear of the Great Unknown.

Inner Earth Dwellers usually fear human beings, remembering how "mystical beings" have been burned at the stake, hanged, stoned to death, or otherwise disposed of, by three dimensional "surface dwellers."

However, if you know and love Gaia, you will identify the vibrations of her Inner Dwellers just as you identify an animal's vibrations.

Many enlightened individuals (star people), find that in a crowd, a stray dog or cat will come to them only. The animal does not sense fear from the star person, and the star person subconsciously "reads" the animal, knowing it is not vicious or rabid.

Many people have the initial fear, "What if this animal hurts me?" This feeling comes without any reason, it is a primitive response which shows their awareness has not developed highly in this sense. The star person's first response is one of empathy and concern for the animal, not fear, and the animal "reads" this in return.

Other-dimensional Inner Dwellers will be drawn to you in the same way, just as you may have already had an experience with a fairy, elf, or nature spirit.

Inner Dwellers vary tremendously in appearance, so we will not attempt to describe who specifically might be drawn to you in these times of upheaval deep within the planet; fairies, elves, and nature spirits are examples of three Inner Dwellers.

However, these three races live part time on the surface as well, whereas some Inner Dwellers never come to the surface unless forced to by critical conditions.

The other-dimensional beings of whom I speak, are not from hell, they are not demons coming out of the earth! To perceive them in this way means there is work needed on raising your own frequency.

If one of the very few negative Inner Dwellers is encountered, simply go the other way, close your mind to them. Blink them out of existence. Most demons dwell in the human mind and spirit, not within Mother Earth.

Let's focus attention again on the Inner Dwellers of Earth: they would rather stay away from the surface and from humankind, but they have no choice at this time. This is still another component of what we call the Change Times.

You have no choice, either, in that you are bound to meet other-dimensional beings in the days ahead.

Look forward with intelligence and warmth, to meeting other members of the universal community. Remember The Third and Fifth Rays of Consciousness, and how their frequency must be raised at this time.

I offer this pre-knowledge so that there is little surprise for you when it happens. We do not want you to experience the kind of surprise which makes you draw back or run away.

It is perfectly natural to feel a bit of "holding back" when one first perceives a very different being; even at the zoo, when you first view a very exotic animal, you just stand there for a moment, perceiving.

How is this animal so strange? Have you never seen a nose like that? Where are the eyes? And what an unusual color and plumage! Before you draw close to his enclosure, you study him intuitively and logically to make sure he is not of bad intent.

Most life forms simply want to live. So it is with nearly all Inner Earth Dwellers. They are not mindless killers or demonic maniacs.

In fact, humankind has managed in these dark ages to offer the most mindless killers and maniacs of any race in the galaxy, including Inner Earth Dwellers.

But, the human race also manages to come up with individuals of great bravery, decency, and spiritual tenacity. The potential of the human race is tremendous if only it can "grow up!"

The Mother Planet is firing up her volcanic furnaces, and the tunnels, cones, and tubes will no longer be useable for living or for teleportation. Though they are other-dimensional, these races cannot live in molten lava, a natural substance which traverses dimensions.

When volcanoes explode, other dimensional-beings are affected the same as you would be; the dimensions share common ground when "pure nature" is the setting.

This is why you may well have a psychic or spiritual experience when you take a hike in a remote, wild forest. Humankind's vibrations are not there in that timeless world, a world which other dimensions know and perceive as clearly as you do.

Pure nature is always a shared intersect point with other dimensions.

I give you this knowledge because to consciously understand what is happening is half the battle. Or, put another way, to consciously understand what is happening, is halfway there, to the risen frequency of the Seven Rays of Consciousness of the Healing Millennium which awaits us.

May the healing light of goodness surround you, always,
Tibus

An Earth Sprite

Artist: Lynn Kvistad

CHAPTER SIXTEEN:
AN ANGEL SPEAKS

This is Shensa-Ray. I come to you in a rainbow of enlightenment.

I am best described as from the Angelic Realm, but I wish you to know that our realm is much broader in its boundaries than humankind has been led to believe.

One of the criteria which can be applied when trying to define our realm, is that we do not live normal life spans by current Terran standards.

When you stop to ponder this, you already know that angels live seemingly immortal lifetimes. This is not literally accurate because nothing and no one is immortal, except for the Creator Spirit which breathes life into all of us.

But, to humans, our life spans would seem to go on, forever.

Another criteria which can be applied to our realm is that we are spiritually oriented. "Spirit" dominates our reality. We do not have three dimensional highways, factories, or houses. There is no need.

Among other "missing" items in our reality, is the three dimensional world's emphasis on sexuality.

Oh, we do have love making. But we do not think of it unless it is part of a very deep love. We do not have sex for the sake of having sex.

Love making is one way of showing our deep love for another's life force.

This is very hard to explain: We do not morally condemn having sex for self gratification. It simply doesn't enter our heads or hearts, just as being able to fly does not realistically enter human minds.

We do feel that "having sex" is very impractical, especially in the late days of the old dark millennium with the threat of AIDS and other diseases, and with the threat of pregnancy which is often not wanted.

Young ones are the greatest gift from The Creator which can be given, but in a dark, over-populated world dominated by money and greed, there is often not a place for another young one to come to Earth.

This channeling mechanism is very difficult! My original point: We of the Angelic Realms are not the way we are because of moral laws or rules. We are the way we are, because this is how we are!

Our spiritual frequency is very high. Each of the Seven Rays of our consciousness sing and shine in a high octave. It is natural for us, there is no other way of being.

Organized religions the world 'round, have made the mistake of trying to legislate and enforce morality.

No wonder love making, for instance, has gotten so jaded. Perversions occur frequently; sex for money, and money given to "buy a place in heaven" are but two of many.

The human being is very rebellious by nature, and churches should have known this. Ah, but perhaps they did and simply took advantage of this fact, making humans pay money for their "sins." And, making them swear allegiance to one narrow way of believing in exchange for "being saved."

We of the Angelic Realm resent (and that is a very angry word for us), the fact that organized religions have attempted to put a "stamp" on us as being their possession only.

In the Dark Millennium, Angels and The Church have gone hand in hand. Churches have known that we have great power and influence with humankind, and so they have tried to hold us captive as their own property. They have tried to use our natural power, and hold it over the people, for their benefit.

Now I am arriving at the crux of my message: Expect to meet an angel. Be ready to encounter the Angelic Realm. No, you need not "go to heaven" to meet us. We are coming to you in these Change Times!

Our presence, the lifting of the veil which has parted us from Terran humanity, is an important event within The Change Times and the risen frequency of the Seven Rays of Consciousness.

However, before we come to you, we must have you understand us as we truly are. Do not automatically connect us with this church or that. This is something we fear, because this is not the time in history to give omnipotence organized religion.

That would be counterproductive, a step backward for you personally. Eventually, your mind and soul will not survive the high frequencies of the Healing Millennium. These energies will drive you insane, your mind will go into oblivion, if it cannot handle them.

If a devout Catholic encounters one of us, she will give credit to The Church. If a devout Baptist encounters the same angel, he will give credit to his church. If a devout Moslem encounters the same angel, he will narrow himself further into his line of belief. This tunneling into one's own church or religion is what The Change Times is not about!

Each of you is free to believe as he or she wishes, but we do not wish to build old walls higher simply by our appearance.

We hope that we of The Angelic Realm will be given "credit" for our appearances and our reality. This is all we ask. The days are over when we are perceived as messengers of The Vatican or representatives of The Methodist Council (or whoever).

We wish to help unite humanity, not split it further. No, not to unite it into the sinister, political, "One World Order." We are aware of this concept but it is far outside of our vibration. Please push it outside of your reality as well. I simply mean, we do not wish to add to religious walls and prejudices.

And so, for the Angelic Realm to manifest and make ourselves known to humankind (as The Change Times dictates we must), we must be sure those enlightened people whom we would choose to appear to, really know who and what we are, giving credit for our existence to The Creator Spirit, and no other narrow, fading, doctrine.

Please give thought and feeling to who, exactly, an angel is.

Yes, we are of a high frequency.

No, we are not three dimensional but can manifest as a three dimensional being.

We are of the spirit, not of the material world.

We are not of the world of immediate gratification.

We are at home in the coming millennium, known as The Healing Millennium. This is our home frequency.

We are beings who are very old by your standards; but, we have "young ones" too, of course. All are wanted and loved, unconditionally.

Immortal? Yes, as much as any being is.

Our natural form is that of a **light form** but we are also a **life form.**

We are not and never have been, exclusively attached to any one religion.

We dwell in a dimension known as The Angelic Realm (there are actually many angelic dimensions). The particular angelic dimension from which I come, is within Terra's domain.

If humankind succeeds in destroying the Mother Planet, he will destroy my world as well.

You might be wondering the following: Yes, there are angels from other planets whom we might call "space angels." Some of the star guardians of star people are these, otherwise known as "guardian angels."

However, to begin discussing this would get me far off the subject. Suffice to say, what I am transmitting applies to space angels as well.

We are not subject to "time." That is why we seem to be immortal. We stand, alive and loving, outside of Time.

Some of us have lived as human beings at some point, then managed to evolve into our current dimension. Others of us are inherently light forms (angels) and have not been human.

I will not try to elaborate on the sub-realms within our larger Realm. That would be off the subject and require a book of its own.

The prime motivation of all angels, regardless of specific realm, is to help, especially at this point in Terran history as the dark days close, and the glorious new dimension awaits us all.

We have what humans call "supernatural powers" with which to help. These include healing abilities which are extremely powerful by human standards.

We also have gifts of precognition, prophesy, telekinesis, levitation, teleportation, and flight, as well as other qualities which are miraculous to humans. As humanity evolves spiritually, these gifts will be given to you as well.

Yes, many of us have wings. Even so, it is more the gifts of levitation and teleportation which make us fly, rather than our sometimes impractical wings. But they are beautiful!

My name has to do with the colorful appearance of my wings, incidentally. I have seven shades of beautiful blue in my wings, from light sky blue to very deep indigo. It is a blessing I was born with, just as you are born with lovely hair. Also, my name encompasses the unique way my wings are formed and shaped.

I ask only that you perceive us for ourselves. Our Angelic Realm is our own world, our own dimension. We are not the possessions of any one religion. You must break away from this belief, and you must do so now. Time is short.

We come closer to possessing Christ Consciousness than beings from many other dimensions do.

Each of us has our own spiritual and karmic background, thus some of us are more Christian oriented than others. Some of us find our foundations and vibrations to be of other religions; others of us are not oriented to Terran religions at all. We simple are.

And what we are, is angels!

It might be advantageous and interesting for you to compare an angel to a human being, trait for trait, so as to perceive the difference.

Then, perceive what we have in common.

We are all life forms of The Creator. We are brothers. We are sisters, to one another. We might be thought of as older sisters and brothers to you humans.

The time is soon coming when we will manifest before you and the veil will be lifted. We look forward to this tremendously!

May the Creator bless you and surround you with Infinite Love,
Shensa-Ray

CHAPTER SEVENTEEN:
THE VOICE OF SASQUATCH

This is the one often called Sasquatch. My true name is Juja.

I send this transmission with the best of intentions and all gestures of peace.

There are many other names for "my kind" which the dominant human species has given us over the ages. "Bigfoot" and "The Abominable Snowman" are two such names. I do not like these names.

My communication will not be complicated like Mr. Tibus' and Mr. Veritan's, because I am not as "smart" as they. I am reaching you, Ms Tessman, through my high degree of telepathic ability, similar to what your felines have. But on your human "IQ tests" I would not do well. I might register as "learning challenged" but in my own world, out in the wilds of Mother Nature, I do perfectly well. And more importantly, my motives are completely peaceful and benign.

I understand that recently it was officially announced that two other species of "Man" lived side by side with Homo sapiens for thousands of years. Me, my wife, my children, my relatives and my ancestors are from one of those "other species of Man." I am your brother.

I also understand that until very recently, Homo sapiens was told by his leaders, that he alone walked Earth, having no real connection or mutual time shared on the planet with other human species. I am sorry Homo sapiens was so badly misled.

For several thousand years of recent history, our lives have been protected by what you call "other-dimensional races from Inner Earth" such as The Tuatha de Danann, a wondrous group of beings with whom you are in contact. They are enabling this transmission as well and send their blessings.

Why would we need to be protected, you ask?

We have needed protection from our brother, Homo sapiens. He would have destroyed us, either murdering us in our natural habitats, or chaining us to be taken to "freak" shows and terrible zoos and exhibits.

Why do we have such a dark opinion of our brother? Many sad experiences give us this knowledge, incidents where our children were hunted and killed, tragedies where our habitats were searched, pillaged, and uprooted.

In general, Man destroys the environment of the entire planet, chasing us from place to place, pushing us into ever more hostile environs.

In the "early days" when three races of Man existed, it was Homo sapiens who became the worshipper of technology which he himself created. Yes, he was and is very "smart," we admit that. We are no match for him!

Homo sapiens became greedier and greedier for "money," and for power, both of which we readily admit, we have no comprehension. We do not understand the worth of this money stuff any more than your pet dog understands "money." But (like your canine friend), we do understand love, compassion, gentleness, and peace.

For all his intellect, it seemed then as it seems now, our brother Homo sapiens does not understand or value these qualities.

But now we hope so fervently that Homo sapiens is, at long last, learning these precious qualities and truths.

Does he think that he cannot have great intellect if he becomes loving, compassionate, gentle, and peaceful?

Certainly he can see the examples of our treasured friends, The Tuatha De Danann, of Tibus and Veritan, of Jesus Christ, of the Angelic realm, of many other great beings, who are intellectually much-blessed (far more than I), but who also display love, compassion, gentleness, and peace.

I understand that tabloid newspapers often run articles on us because Homo sapiens is very curious about us. Do we exist, and what we are like if we are real?

Recently a zoologist told of his nine days in the Washington State wilderness; we helped him after he sprained his ankle, and apparently he said we treated him "like a king."

My friends The Tuatha De Danann explain to me that this is a great compliment, meaning we were gentle and considerate with him.

But, of course we were! We have no "kings" who control this stuff called "power," and "money," we have never had the need for this. This is a need of Homo sapiens, involved with his lust for "owning" more and more.

We, on the other hand, we treat any brother or sister well, should he or she be given to us by the universe, to care for.

We have cared for stray kittens and puppies, stray cats and dogs, for as long as I can remember. Often these are abandoned by our brother Homo sapiens for some incomprehensible reason.

My friends the Tuatha De Danann have also explained to Juja (that's me), that Homo sapiens developed this greed, this urge to exploit and conquer, very long ago. This is why The Tuatha De Danann themselves "turned sideways to the sun" and got as far away from Homo sapiens as they could. They went into "the other place," a place where they sometimes take us, as a protective measure.

The Tuatha De Danann explain to me that the last thousand years in particular have been a very dark phase of God's mind. I celebrate the fact that the wheel turns toward the sunlight now.

My wife is my mate for life and I do love her dearly. Her name is Camie. She was taken to "the other place" not long ago when some Homo sapiens hunters stalked her, nearly murdering her. They were excited to catch a glimpse of "Bigfoot" but human-like, they proceeded to hunt her viciously, trying to murder her.

These actions, I will never understand! My Camie would not have been able to outsmart these hunters, nor outrun them, especially because she was carrying my fifth beautiful daughter in her womb at the time.

The Tuatha De Danann appeared from "no where" as they often do for us, and these true friends took Camie through Our Mother Earth, to the Inner Sanctum, until the vicious hunters left.

We love the other members of our species. Sometimes we males tend to "roughhouse" with each other and become territorial. It is then we see a slight trace of the aggressive Homo sapiens in ourselves. Perhaps this is a beginning evolution, I do not know, but I do hope not! We all vow not to be anything like Homo sapiens.

We chose long ago to live in lone families where no tribal warfare, no competing for "strongest dominant male" could ever take place.

Besides, there are very few of us left, and we need to enhance each other's chances, not hurt them.

Are you surprised The Tuatha de Danann live under the earth in Washington State? They tell me to say, they are not confined to the place called Ireland, it is merely where their roots lie. Before that, they came from the sky.

There is a huge petroglyph, say they, near Horsethief Lake State Park in Washington State called "She Who Watches," and this is a creation of my friends, The Tuatha De Danann, in conjunction with the Native Americans there. This petroglyth looks much like early artwork in the place called Ireland, I am told.

My friends The Tuatha De Danann apologize for taking over the thrust of this transmission for a moment; this transmission, they say, is to be Juja's message, not theirs, and so they will not continue with this "petroglyph" information at this time.

I do know what I, Juga, want to impart: I understand that the time is soon coming when Homo sapiens will meet other-dimensional beings such as The Tuatha De Danann, and beings from the stars overhead. These are beings of whom I have some knowledge and I find them, for the most part, to be kinder than Homo sapiens though a few bad ones have taken members of my people for experimentation.

I also understand that my people may soon have to come face to face with Homo sapiens once again. We will have to face not one individual, but the entire species of Homo sapiens.

Humans will then know what they knew long ago: That we, another species of "Man" still survive!

I also understand that my friends The Tuatha De Danann will protect us, will protect me, should I have to meet Homo sapiens.

We have dreaded Home sapiens for so long, been so frightened of him.

I am so happy to know that Homo sapiens will not be the Homo sapiens which I now know. He will have seen the errors of his ways, the wrongness of his behavior.

I understand Homo sapiens has the ability to learn and to grow. He is so smart, I would think he did have this ability!

I am told Homo sapiens is about to become similar to my friends, The Tuatha De Danann.

I am also told that my people, Homo erectus, are about to take a step forward, that we will gain the "smarts" which Homo sapiens has, but that we will retain our loving and compassionate ways. Our ways have been with us for so long now, I believe we will remain benign; I believe this with all my heart.

Homo sapiens became very aggressive early-on, before he had really grown up at all. He had not learned. Now I believe he is learning!

For this, I give thanks to the Creator of All. We await you, Homo sapiens, our brother, with love, gentleness, compassion, and peace.

Juja

Artist's rendition of Juja
Artist: Merrilee Miller

CHAPTER EIGHTEEN:
CHANTELLA SINGS

This is Chantella.

I come to you as a clear note in the octave above yours, within the cosmic symphony we share.

More and more of us on the Home Side are being urged to communicate with our friends on Earth. Your numbers on Earth are also expanding as more and more enlightened people begin to pursue a star path (spirit path) as opposed to the materialistic, narrow path of the old millennium.

For both groups of us (we are really **one**), it is no longer a luxury to reach out to co-workers on the other side, it is imperative.

My people do not usually communicate in language or even in telepathic concepts. Our communicative skills are in musical tones and notes, whether sung or sent telepathically.

This is difficult to explain, but if you were to meet us, and observe as two of us communicate, then you would understand much better.

In fact, you will meet us, and we will meet you, in The Healing Millennium of the next thousand years. However, our meeting is not in the distant future; all humanity will realize we "aliens" are as real as you are, very soon. This is a large part of what the Change Point is all about.

It is then that it will be safe for us to meet openly, face to face. Until then, it is safe for neither of us.

Channeling to Diane in concepts which have components of words, is difficult for me, just as you might find it difficult to use a foreign language with great skill. Perhaps more accurately, it is like you trying to convey extremely complicated concepts in sign language.

This is because my form of communication does not involve using another language formed through linguistics. This, therefore, is a whole new "base of operations" for my mind. Luckily, I am telepathic by nature.

Oh, I do not aim to belabor this point or to be selfish in taking space. I am only explaining why I must go slowly and meticulously in my transmission. Just a slight nuance can be wrong. If one small word is not sent clearly, it can throw the whole transmission into shambles. This is a responsibility on the part of both receiver (channel) and sender.

I do feel sometimes that human channels are not careful enough in this process, perhaps we on the Home Side are at fault, too. (Chantella wishes to give an example): The channel writes, "Starships are from Venus," when in fact the message was, "Starships are not from Venus." A huge difference of just one small word.

I am endeavoring this transmission not only because I need to learn to communicate conceptually as well as through my native tonal, musical medium, but also because it is the area which is my specialty aboard our ship which now requires an urgent message to be sent to you.

My area of specialty is "the media." That is, how the human mediums of television, films, radio, books, computer communication, advertisements, and so forth, can help introduce into the human mass consciousness, the reality of the existence of aliens, both from space and dimension.

Of course, also inherent in this, is the concept that we are visiting Earth.

I am amongst the "architects" of this media endeavor, I am not one who has directly channeled to such film-makers as Gene Roddenberry and Steven Spielberg, but members of my staff have. Now, it is time for me to communicate directly, too.

Suffice to say, we have telepathically influenced such films as **Close Encounters of the Third Kind** and **Star Trek**, but, there have been films of a similar nature to which we did not have direct in-put.

Humanity is prone to make imitations of "originals;" so, to make money, film makers continue to make "encounter" and "space" films on their own. And this is alright with us. We need plant only a seed of good quality, and then we know other seeds will sprout.

Our one objective is to simply make humans aware that we do exist, not to control your minds as to exactly how we act (indeed, we are very diverse).

The only other thing I must say about my specialty is that we do not "censor" film efforts, nor control film makers' minds.

We also urge that the negative side of extraterrestrial visitors be shown, though these visitors have nothing to do with us. Film makers are then free to make additional films about frightening and evil aliens.

Unfortunately, this "horror genre" makes money, and so the situation becomes unbalanced. Films illustrate many bad aliens when, indeed there are only a few. At this point, we must take a deep sigh.

Now, a matter of urgent concern: The human media has gone somewhat "wild." That is, the media is flooded with things UFO, things psychic, things New Age, and things that go bump in the night.

Some of it is directly inspired from us, much is not. But this is not the point.

Shouldn't we be happy that the ball is rolling so well and fast?

Yes, in the bigger picture, but, the general masses have trouble telling the shaft from the wheat.

An example: Recent UFO and New Age Conferences, featuring a variety of speakers with different points of views, have been poorly attended. People do not bother to drive to conferences anymore, because they can switch on their televisions and see all sorts of "weird stuff" all the time.

How many people simply check the UFO pages on the Internet? Many!

There is nothing wrong with UFO information on The Internet, except that the mode of information tends to dehumanize all of it, forming a comfortable, untouchable barrier between communicators.   I must add, our main concern about the Internet is that, while it was "wild and free" several years ago, huge steps have been made by repressive, sinister agencies to keep track of exactly who is using it and what each contributes. There is not the anonymity which you may think there is, not any more. Be warned.

The television series which feature alien plots seem to be running far afield in order to be sensational and gain high ratings. Again, we do not and cannot control this, we must "let it roll." These are our rules for ourselves.

But, I must beg you: Please, please, be discerning! If a "live" grass roots UFO conference is in town, where you can hear real debate, various opinions, diverse presentations and arguments, go to this!

Read the latest New Age, UFO, or psychic books which appeal to you, which touch your heart, soul, and mind. Delve into the older books on these subjects, they contain invaluable knowledge.

Dig deeper for the truth. Continue to forge your own path. Do not fall victim to every conspiracy theory, but remain open minded.

Continue to keep your eye on the highest star.

The danger is, precious energy may become diffused. This is the same energy which must and will grow to such momentum as to raise the frequency! This is your energy which will create the higher frequency of consciousness of the future in the Healing Millennium.

I am not so much concerned about the many negative views of "us aliens." But, the diffusion of energy at this point, could be fatal for you, and for your planet and her myriad of dimensions.

Too many rumors, too much shallow, egotistical lip service to deep metaphysical concepts, too much greed to "make more money by doing a sequel," all of this and more, threaten to make "extreme strangeness" ho-hum, everyday stuff.

A grass roots conference, for instance, shakes up this complacency as one confronts a legitimate but mind-boggling theory and the enormity of it all. But to simply settle for the next installment of a far-out television series, allows others to guide and control your explorations. What more can they possibly dream up to horrify and shock?

This is not the true Healing Millennium! This is a Dark Millennium "version" of enlightenment. It is a false version.

Perhaps these diffused activities which threaten to make it all every day stuff, are alright for many people. At least it is something beyond the daily routine.

But for those of you reading this, enlightened human friends, do not let this become "enough!" Keep exploring and searching, even if it is more difficult to drive to a conference than to turn on the tv. Stay true to your heart and soul, do not settle for less.

Keep your edge, forge new paths, leap over obstacles.

Yours is a spirit quest as well as a scientific search for the truth.

Yes, the truth is out there! And it is also within. Do not settle for less!

I close with the musical blessings of my people:

May the music of the vast universe sing in your heart.
Chantella

CHAPTER NINETEEN:
THE THREAT OF ARTIFICIAL INTELLIGENCE THROUGH MULTI-DIMENSIONAL COMPUTERS

This is Amethysta. I come to you in the deep purple ray of radiant, unconditional love.

Highly advanced computers are a huge threat to Earth at the close of the Dark Millennium. They constitute "artificial intelligence" in one of its most dangerous forms.

Such computers, by nature, will analyze the "program" of other intelligences, including humankind's intellectual ability. When they do so, they will inevitably conclude that their own intellectual ability is "multi-dimensional," whereas the human being's intellect (he/she who created the computer), is single-dimensional.

We speak of the fact that, at this point in time, humanity does not have the ability to be "of two or more dimensions." Computers, on the other hand, are on the brink of multi-dimensional presence and influence.

We beings of Space/Dimensional Intelligence do have multi-dimensional ability, for instance. It is the ability to have presence in, or impose influence on, other dimensions while still remaining who/where you are in your "home dimension." This is a complicated subject in itself, but I wish to keep the emphasis here on the threat of artificial intelligence.

Once these computers realize that they have gained multi-dimensional ability, they will conclude that they are superior to humanity and that humanity must be "restrained."

Humanity, they will reason, must become their "inferior pet." It did, after all, create the self (the computer), and so will be kept around for a while for reference.

However, if humankind becomes a threat, such as trying to "pull the plug" on these machines, then these computers would turn against their "pet."

This has happened in other advanced technological societies on other worlds, and it can spell death for the race which did the inventing!

Other computers with other capabilities might come to the same conclusion, but we have found in our experience, that this "multi-dimensional" achievement within computers is the most dangerous capability for a computer to possess. This ability proves to the computer mind that it must begin to run its own program and agenda. This is exactly the point at which Earth's advanced computers now find themselves.

Yes, we all can warn Earth's scientists not to pursue this technology. Will they listen? Do they listen to anyone?

Also, we all can pray and meditate on the subject.

However, this cold technical subject is not influenced easily by spiritual energies. It is one of the most difficult areas to change (upgrade) through psychic energy. Computers do not have psychic or spiritual components, because these come from the soul. How can a computer be influenced psychically?

However, the greatest hope is that humankind will soon become multi-dimensional itself through the coming risen frequency of consciousness.

Humankind's transformation of The Seven Rays of Consciousness to their new, higher frequency, will empower your race with powerful psychic gifts.

This is the valid, pure, and natural way of becoming multi-dimensional.

When this happens with humankind, advanced computers will not be "superior" even by their own definition.

But even better, there will be no need for such high technology with such enormous capability. Computers will not run the show in the Healing Millennium; they are far too important in the final years of the old millennium.

Computers will be extinct just as the governments who use them.

Do angels live in a world run by computers? Do we of the Space/Time Intelligence give computers power over our lives? The answer to both questions is an emphatic, "No!"

Humanity cannot become multi-dimensional through technology, because doomsday would follow as certainly as if computers gained control. What is lacking in the human race is its spiritual development.

Humanity must raise its spiritual frequency; it is imperative from so many different aspects and angles.

It is the only solution and the only door to The Future!

I shower you with deep purple healing rays, and bless you.

Amethysta

NOTE ON AMETHYSTA'S IDENTITY

We first heard from Amethysta in the early 1990s. I received a report from a woman who had encountered a UFO which had landed in the snow; she had also seen small beings with large eyes outside the craft, examining the snow, and playing in it! She felt completely safe and at peace to watch them, and felt they knew of her presence. This woman and I became good friends, which was an added bonus.

Several weeks after this incident, she felt she received channeled messages from one of these little beings whose name was Amethysta. Her new telepathic friend was from a far distant planet and had been experiencing "Earth snow" for the first time the night of the UFO experience.

Shortly after that, I was thrilled to receive a channeled message from one who identified herself as "the same Amethysta," and this delightful female alien has since become a steady contributor to my various channeled endeavors.

CHAPTER TWENTY:
THE VIBRATION OF DIANA LUMINATIS

This is Diana Luminatis. I adorn you with light.

First, allow me to explain that I am not Princess Diana who died so tragically. However, the essence of the lovely being who was/is Princess Diana has joined with the "home vibration" of the Diana Luminatis archetype, who is me. This is a difficult reality to explain in current Earth language but I shall try:

There is an old saying: You cannot imagine what you cannot imagine. My existence lies just on the fringe of humanity's present ability, to conceive of me, and then to perceive me.

There are higher beings within the cosmos, who are "larger than life" but who do contain the "soul stuff" of great humans on Earth. This "soul stuff" can and does come to us from a number of brilliantly shining human beings. Thus, their persona is reflected within us, and we are reflected within them during their lifetimes.

These human beings have reached a point in their spiritual evolution wherein they can embrace Life itself, becoming a "bigger than life" individual, rather than coming back in human form again. Another way of saying "a bigger than life being" is to consider us as "archetypes." Carl Jung introduced this term as a means of expressing a "mass consciousness role model" which the whole human race can embrace.

A young human boy chooses a baseball player as an individual role model, but the young human race chooses, among others, "Diana Luminatis" as a role model; therefore, I echo deep in the mass consciousness. Another example of an individual who embodied my vibration was Queen Gwenivere of the King Arthur legends.

When you as a spiritual seeker first go in search of your own guardian angel, you will often identify him or her with a human archetype.

You may perceive your guardian angel as a component of the Diana Luminatis archetype. Or, your guardian may appear to you as a dashing Robin Hood type, or a Joan of Arc spiritual persona, or a Mother Mary image. Or even as Jesus-like. There are many examples, all cherished by the human race.

I want to stress that we "archetype beings" are very real and alive unto ourselves in the higher realms. We are not just an image or projection of human hopes and fears. We are _all_ of the above.

That we archetypical beings are real and alive as well, is a revolutionary concept to the modern human race, and one which takes a while to accept.

However, ancient humans knew us well, and this is how legends from Hercules to Thor, were born. Apollo, Diane of the Hunt, Athena, Count St. Germaine, Moses, the examples are many.

After the Change Point, this will all be clear and natural to your perception, my friend.

Princess Diana had found something very special within herself in recent years, something which allowed her to know that her spiritual energy was/is a part of myself, Diana Luminatis.

Princess Diana was not aware of this spiritual aspect of herself until she "bottomed out" following a suicide attempt. She rebounded with renewed strength, beauty, and spiritual purpose. My people always wish to help others, and this was also her wish.

You will know from your own experiences that you find great spiritual truth and inspiration within yourself just when things are darkest. It is then The Light shines through. Regardless of the earthly cause of Princess Diana's passing on Earth, it was/is time on Earth's cosmic clock, for me, Diana Luminatis, archetype and living being of The Light, to become empowered. I am awakening once again.

Do not grieve for Princess Diana. It is most painful for her sons who are left behind, but they are strong young men who will become influential in Earth's rising frequency; they will know that their mother did not die, but that she moved onward, to live in The Light.

I ask you, my friend in The Light, to consider your own guardian angel or spirit guide in terms of "what archetype does he or she fit?" King Arthur? Nostradamus? Joan of Arc? Morgeanna? Jesus of Nazareth? Lancelot? Count St. Germaine? Mother Mary? Ashtar? Robin Hood? Einstein? Even Capt. Kirk, Mr. Spock, or Luke Skywalker?

Do not laugh, my friend. These are the role models of Homo sapiens, but do you know that there are also living beings of The Light who fit the characteristics attributed to each of these persona? Indeed there are.

Some I have mentioned once lived on Earth, others are originally fictional characters, or that is what their legend-creators thought as they wrote about them and channeled their messages.

In our realm, we have come into existence in many ways and not all of us have lived as a specific human being; "beinghood" is more complex than humanity dreams it to be. One can reach beinghood in a number of amazing ways. We archetypical beings are not "mass minds" such as bees and ants even though our "soul stuff" is usually a joining of many like-souls.

The nature of our beinghood will soon become natural for you to comprehend and perhaps, of which to be a part. We are "bigger than life beings" composed of many outstanding, enlightened souls, often from Earth's historical timelines. Outstanding, enlightened individuals often come from us, and return to us.

I wish to add here that not all guardian angels or spirit contacts conveniently fit the image of a specific archetype; therefore, do not worry if your spirit guide does not seem to have an archetypical image within your mind and heart. However, as these days of "Old Earth" grow very short, it is important to have a conceptual image of your guardian, a psychic indicator of his or her frequency.

I am much pleased that Elton John's "Good-bye England's Rose" lyrics were written in such a way as to link Princess Diana with The Land, which is in this particular incident, England. It is reminiscent of the King Arthur legend's magical connection to The Land.

This truly links the Diana persona with Gaia, the living spirit of Mother Earth. I, Diana Luminatis, am infinitely and proudly linked to Mother Earth.

In these troubled days, my persona is awakened, and spreads across The Land, to protect, to bless, to heal, and then to evolve with her.

I AM   Diana Luminatis

"HYMN TO DIANA LUMINATIS"

Your image stands out in the lake. In your left hand, you hold the torch of Enlightenment. Its flame flickers over the black waters like oil afire. With your right hand, you clasp the bow, yet a doe seeks shelter at your side. I understand and venerate your mystery, protectress of animals, mistress of the hunt. From your fair face, you gaze down compassionately into the depths. You behold all their secrets. Lady of the Night, protect our sacred lake! Bless its indwelling spirits and grant us, the living, the enlightenment of your love.

-- Roman priest of Diana at Ostia, late 3rd century

Archetypical Beings

Artist: Merrilee Miller

CHAPTER TWENTY-ONE
THE VOLCANO GODDESS' WARNING

This is B'Tamei and I am a Gaian Spirit.

Greetings to all receiving this transmission. You may also think of me as a nature spirit. I have been referred to by many names by various segments of the human race for thousands of years, but to make matters clear, you may simply think of me as the Goddess of the Volcano. I am the spirit which drives the volcano.

I dwell in the many volcanic cones, tubes, and mountains all across my Mother Planet and these structures worship and celebrate me in their unique way.

I remind you that I am not a "good" entity, but I am not a "bad" entity, either. I am an amoral entity, the living spirit of the volcano.

I take life if it in my way but I do not seek to take life. I merely seek to exist and to give vent to pent up energies which cannot be held within the depths of our Mother Planet.

As this anger is vented, my ego manifests. I become conscious, a living energy, whose body is the molten lava which rolls in a magnificent manner down the mountainside; the image of my form may also be perceived in the thick volcanic ash which encompasses the air for hundreds of miles. Once in a while, I manifest as a beautiful, exotic woman just above the volcano's cone, the Goddess of the Volcano.

New Zealand natives have spotted me as a gorgeous, vaporous woman floating just above Mt. Ruapehu on several occasions just within the last year. In 1996 and 1997, Sicily's Mount Etna and I embraced, and streams of molten lava spilled from the northeast crater. Due to my living spirit, the mountain left his dormant sleep, and through him, I also came alive. Ours is a symbiotic relationship.

Humans, you must perceive what "spirit" truly is! You must also perceive that many other beings possess "spirit" besides you! Some of these beings originate in a totally different fashion from your physical birth process.

Sicily is a very mystical island; even your (human) Mafia started there as a secret, mystical group which was to defend its people from outside oppressors. Mount Etna and I constantly provide Sicily with a mystical thrill which reaches the spirits and hearts of the Sicilian people. So it is with human beings who live close to me in various locations all over the globe; they know me as a living entity.

Life on Earth is dull without such natural cataclysmic thrills, is it not? We nature spirits may be dangerous to you humans but we also do great good for your heart and soul; we energize! We remind you that when things get bad enough that you have to struggle for survival, it is then you are most alive.

Our natural pyrotechnics are visible for many miles; it is glorious. And what pleasure venerable "Old Faithful," the ageless geyser of Yellow Stone in America gives you! Or the rampaging water spirit of Niagara Falls? Yes, we re-charge the human spirit.

Why does modern man not see us as we are? You are slaves of the scientific approach, and thus you omit the most vital, vibrant part of yourself from the scenario, and out of your life. You fail to perceive "spirit."

There is now increased volcanic activity across the planet; our ring of fire has awakened! Prepare, beware, but also, anticipate!

Our global ring of fire would not have awakened if humankind had not hurt and thus angered our Mother Earth. At least, it would not have awakened with the vengeance which is now occurring.

Humankind has nearly killed its Mother Planet, no wonder she is giving vent to so much negative emotion! I am honored to be the expression of this emotion, because it cannot be held in any longer. I am helping her.

You see evidence of her negative emotion also in the great number of hurricanes which ravage your shores. Lashua is my friend, the Goddess of the Hurricane. And now, "the child" El Nino visits you.

The Mother Planet also manifests typhoons which are, to her, only a slightly different way of emotional expression.

However, Earth spirits can be reached, we can be reasoned with.

Our Mother Earth, can also be reached and reasoned with. Every consciousness in the universe wishes some kind of recognition by others. In Earth's case, she was/is your mother, and yet modern humankind has failed to even recognize her existence as a living entity.

Our Mother Earth looks in humanity's mirror of perception, and she fails to see herself! Yet, humankind is her child. You dominate the planet but do not reflect Mother Earth, who gave you life and spirit. Humanity must "admit" that you are indeed a part of Nature! You must perceive your Mother Planet as an entity, just as you did in ancient times.

I need not list what is physically wrong with Earth which is man-made, everything from the diminishing ozone layer to the rain forests being decimated. Large chunks of remaining rainforest have recently been sold to Far Eastern logging companies; the scene grows worse!

You see, emotion and spirit are intertwined with "the physical," even where a planetary soul is concerned. You know how your own physical health is related to your emotional state. It is the same with your planet.

You must work spiritually with Gaia as never before, my enlightened human friend. Also, engage in environmental activism on the physical level.

While I find a great release in volcanic eruptions, we do not wish to do this indefinitely. Every spirit needs to rest.

I will rejoice in a new spiritual dimension, as will you, because humans and other beings, will perceive and communicate with me, The Volcano Goddess. You will "give me my due" as a living spirit; this has not been the case for a very long time. "Modern man" and volcano spirits simply do not have much in common.

But those who embrace mysticism as well as science, those who revel in spirit as well as logic, will perceive me and know me. For this I will give thanks!

Remember, the atoms which make up your body, were freed from the bowels of the Earth, by me. Volcanoes send new atoms onto the surface. Yes, all that is you physically was once in a volcano!

I also remind you that the surface of Earth would be flat as a pancake and smooth as a marble without volcanic activity. You see, I am not all bad.

Meanwhile, I advise you not to settle on any volcanic slopes, be they "dormant" or active! I do not wish to fill the entire planet's sky with ash and cause widespread climate upheaval in this way. Please communicate with me, even help me!

I am B'Tamei

AN ADDITIONAL TRANSMISSION FROM B'TAMEI

In regard to the Caribbean island of Montserrat and her Soufriere Hills Volcano, you must be thinking, "What kind of monster is this so-called goddess?"

Montserrat used to be an exceptionally beautiful island. Now that island is virtually destroyed by Soufriere, who has come alive with a vengeance. My spirit is indeed powerful within the very angry Soufriere.

Even the so-called "safe" north end of Montserrat is nearly uninhabitable these days as Soufriere continues to demonstrate just an iota of Mother Nature's potential power, a power which can just as easily affect any and every corner of this planet.

With the Soufriere Hills eruptions come many earthquakes; quakes are on the rise all over the world. When the oldest of you were children, there were a score of earthquakes worldwide each year, give or take a few. Now there are thousands of quakes each year.

Some say it is simply that more careful records are made possible through modern technology but I assure you, there are hundreds, even thousands, more earthquakes happening now than a few short years ago.

Need I mention the earthquakes in Italy which seemed determined to wipe out the religious building dedicated to Francis of Assisi. Tremors struck this ancient structure again and again causing much damage. It is sad that the building which has sustained so much damage is named after a very caring human, Francis of Assisi.

In the late summer of 1997, earthquakes rocked Bangladesh, Israel, Iran, Taiwan, San Francisco, the Palm Springs area, Australia suffered the strongest quake in a decade, the state of Nebraska, Tibet, Tokyo, Turkey, various areas of South America, Indonesia, the city of Seattle, and South Africa; there have been numerous small but unusual tremors along eastern Tennessee, the Tennessee/Georgia border, and also in Kentucky. These are but a few of the recent quake areas.

May I return to the subject of awakening volcanoes? There will be many more volcanic fireworks and millions of humans worldwide will have ringside seats to these eruptions.

When is "show time?" It may be anytime, anywhere. Volcanoes are awakening which you do not even know to be volcanic cones.

The 17,000 foot Popocatepetl continues to spew ash and poisonous gas toward 20 million Mexican homes. She has the power to explode with the force of

10,000 atomic bombs.

Humankind has done great damage to our Mother's ozone layer with his nuclear bomb testing; it was this layer which was our Mother's immune system. Humankind has also hurt himself and fellow lifeforms with his nuclear stupidity. Today he is finding out that in the 1950s, there were "hot spots" all over the world as the result of the Nevada atom bomb tests.

Many humans themselves now suffer with, (for instance), thyroid cancer as a result of this childhood exposure. I only wish that the specific humans who developed and sanctioned that terrible testing would be their own victims.

Alas, this is seldom the case. Even the Nazi death doctor Mengele died an exceptionally easy death, suffering a stroke as an old man, then falling beneath the waves to drown quickly.

My spirit is also strong within Vesuvius, that legendary volcano which contributed to the rise and fall of great human civilizations of the past. Vesuvius looms over Naples and other populated areas, home to eleven million people, and this mighty volcano is catnapping no more. The Mother Planet has called on her to wake up!

Humans have, with their usual lack of foresight, moved onto the sides of many of Earth's fifteen hundred active volcanoes in this modern era.

The human race is over-populating Earth at an alarming rate, and wouldn't you know they would move right onto the sides of volcanoes? The huge city Tokyo stands in the shadow of an active volcano, as do Seattle and Tacoma, Washington.

It was not so long ago by my standards of telling time, that volcanic mudslides swept through the places where both these U.S. cities stand.

On November 13, 1985, 26,000 people died who had moved onto the fertile slopes of an ice-capped volcano in the mountains of Columbia. The people felt they were safe, living thirty or forty miles away.

The exploding ice cap picked up debris and mud as it roared down the side of the mountain. I need not complete this story.

Mother Earth still has more power, wounded though she may be by humankind, than this selfish race can possibly imagine. "Disaster films" don't begin to show the Mother Planet's full potential.

But, enough of my "boasting." I must sound downright evil. I assure you, I am not. Like Mother Nature herself, I can be extremely generous and giving; just look at the fertile slopes which surround volcanoes. This is land which abounds with life. Yes, I can be destructive. When I am this way, I do not do so with the intentional purpose of being cruel or of hurting or killing. I am angry; I must (literally) let off steam. Pressure builds, and I am indeed a powerful force. I perceive this each time I see the damage I have done.

I know I harm wildlife and flora as well as humans; please understand, I do not explode with the conscious intention of destroying life. I merely explode, period. This is similar to when you are done an injustice and become angry without planning to be angry.

Remember as you seek to understand what I say, that you are a physical being and a spiritual being. In the same way, Earth is a physical being and a spiritual being.

The physical cause of a volcanic eruption is pressure that has built up in volcanic tubes from within the Earth.

But, the spiritual reason for this pressure is that Earth is hurt, angry, weakened, depressed, and worried about her future existence.

If someone had done a grave injustice to you, your physical blood pressure would rise, but you would be spiritually hurt, angry, depressed, weakened, and worried about your future. It would help you to vent your emotions; otherwise, you might suffer a breakdown.

Would it not be beneficial if a loving soul communicated with you, alleviating your anger, cleansing your hurt, explaining that in the future (a Risen Earth), you would be loved and cared about? This loving soul would acknowledge his link to you and thank you for giving him birth.

For several thousand years, almost no one has acknowledged the entity which is Mother Earth as deserving of love, or even acknowledged her beinghood. You already know what I am going to beg you to do. You must spiritually and psychically work with Gaia, the living spirit of Mother Earth.

Intensify your efforts to alleviate her anger, to cleanse and heal her wounds. If you want a world on which to stand, on which to live, you must do this! If it is possible, also please communicate with me, the Spirit of the Volcano and/or the entity which manifests before, during and after earthquakes whom we might call the Spirit of the Quake.

You will not be able to stop all the destruction but we are capable of sending and receiving communication through the common link of consciousness. We are capable of being calmed.

You, my enlightened human friend, have consciousness. We, the Earth spirits, have consciousness. Gaia herself has consciousness, and she is also your mother. Of course you can communicate with her! Of course you can help her! Mother Earth is also our mother. Therefore, we are cosmic siblings, you and us. Of course you can communicate with us!

Do not be as humankind has been before you, feeling that you are the only one with consciousness, believing that there is a "blank wall" if you attempt communication with beings other than other humans.

I feel I have pleaded my case as adequately as I can. You may wonder, if I am amoral, why do I care to make this plea, and how can I do this as a rational being? Am I not a wild spirit, probably not attuned to wording concepts involving love and decency? I have a higher self just as you do, you see. I can strive to communicate as the higher realms do; I have certain knowledge that I am climbing upward on the cosmic evolutionary ladder.

Star guardian friends assist me in these communications, perhaps "civilizing" my words and emotions, but the basis of what I say, of what I beg of you, comes from my heart and soul, through that presence known as my higher self.

B'Tamei

CHAPTER TWENTY-TWO:
NUCLEAR TERRORISM

This is R'Lu'Xon. I come to you in the light of good intent.

My name is not important but still I perceive Diane sitting at the keyboard for at least ten of your minutes trying to make out what I am sending in the way of a "name." Perhaps slightly more important is the fact I am a scientist with the Space/Dimensional Intelligence of which our friend Tibus and other good beings, are members.

My specialty in regard to Earth is the nuclear threat, and I possess an expertise regarding nuclear energy. This expertise is not used actively when I work with our own projects, because we do not make use of nuclear energy. We do not want it, not ever! Therefore, I also have another scientific specialty also for which I was originally educated. My education began on my home planet but has continued throughout my career with Space/Dimensional Intelligence. My home planet can be perceived when you look into the night skies at the constellation Delphinius. I am most concerned with the growing possibility of human terrorists using nuclear weapons. Facilities containing materials for making nuclear weapons are not guarded sufficiently in a number of places, all over the world.

As you know, just a small amount of radioactive plutonium, for instance, can contaminate and kill over a wide area; the entire planet would be adversely affected to some degree also. When will you learn, nuclear radiation is anti-life!

In Russia, there is a stockpile of fourteen hundred tons of nuclear material. These facilities are pitifully unsupervised, and are not well guarded or locked. We have managed to bring this to the attention of the mass media, because the media is very powerful on Earth. So, you may have recently heard on your evening television news that in 1996, the United States paid for a burglar alarm to be installed at one Russian facility.

In many of these facilities, uranium is just sitting around, "for the taking." I wish you to know that we do keep watch on these facilities through our technical surveillance ability so that we know what is happening at them. However, it is not always easy for us to act as "police person" when there is a theft. Obviously we must be creative because we cannot, being three foot tall humanoid aliens (as some of us are), put on a police uniform and cap to arrest the terrorists. And to what prison are we to take them?

I am being facetious, but basically, these are our problems. Also, we cannot go about interfering with the natural course of physical events on Earth. We do attempt to influence humans spiritually as I am attempting to do right now.

We will also send psychic messages to a pivotal individual once in a while which attempt to influence the course of human history if the situation is very grave. However, we "good guys" do this as little as possible. This is still interference. We never use our psychic powers for actual mind control. If mind control is involved, an individual is in contact with negative beings.

The nuclear terrorist threat is one of the gravest concerns involving nuclear energy in the final years of the Dark Millennium. We also have grave concerns about China's willingness to use atomic weapons (supplied by the United States), against the west coast of the United States. Obviously this has the potential for a huge disaster. Taiwan is a constant bone of contention between these two powers. Of course, Iraq and North Korea continue to be threats to the entire world's life force; the people of these two countries are near starvation in many cases, and still the rulers continue their egotistical, power hungry paths.

Why am I bothering to send this message when there is little you personally can do, it would seem, to solve these situations? One reason is, I wish you to know that if you have a strong psychic intuitive feeling **not** to go to a place or event which has thousands of people, you should follow that feeling and not go.

This is a very tricky piece of advice because the power of suggestion can make an individual not go to a number of places, which would have been perfectly safe to go to. We do not want fear to rule.

However, at this point, if you do have a clear, strong premonition or "gut level" feeling, then do not go. This is one little bit of protection for you. This also assists you in developing your own psychic powers of precognition which will be yours once the frequency has been raised.

If you are in contact with your guardian and/or spirit guides, they will attempt to send psychic warnings to you also, if such a threat exists.

Second, the psychic power of the planet's enlightened individuals is stronger than you might possibly imagine. You can lessen the possibility of thermonuclear war or terrorist nuclear bombings through your spiritual/psychic efforts.

Your psychic power, when combined with that of many other good, enlightened individuals, multiplies exponentially. Think about examples in history: It takes relatively few brave souls to initiate drastic change in a society. This is true more than ever before, on the path leading to the Healing Millennium.

It is more difficult to influence governments and terrorists psychically than Mother Earth or natural entities who are more spiritually inclined. But, you must know that you can help lessen the possibility of a terrible nuclear disaster occurring. Please work on this urgent concern in your prayers and meditations.

Positive thought waves do help create a reality in which this threat never manifests. Never underestimate your consciousness' influence on the entire world's reality! It would not hurt at this point in The Change Times, to increase your "disaster supply" of food, water, medical supplies, tools, whatever emergency provisions you need. Most aware individuals do have a basic supply. Don't forget supplies for your animal friends as well.

In the case of nuclear terrorism, the radioactive contamination might not be great enough in your area to threaten your life, as long as you have a pre-existing supply of food and water. That is, as long as you do not have to go out and buy newly contaminated items. So, be well supplied. This is helpful for natural disasters as well which may well be happening as the climate changes drastically.

I am scientifically based, my planet's people are of this orientation. But I am a good soul who recognizes the reality and necessity of spiritual growth and high awareness. I never harm other life forms or other worlds. I work for enlightenment and progress, both technical and spiritual.

For a race's accomplishments to "qualify" as true technical progress, technology has to be controlled and harnessed by the spiritual nature inherent in that race. Spirit must lead! It is for this spiritual reason that I work with the Space/Time Intelligence which is attempting to help you, help yourselves. We hope so desperately to save your world.

In order to save as many alternate realities of your world as possible, we must work in each of these multi-dimensions. In other words, your current reality may be one which is a disastrous "9" on the Reality Continuum, but you can "hook into" the reality which is a "4". You can make this your home reality.

How can you do this? This entire book guides you on "how to."

You can avoid the terrible "9" cataclysmic reality, and move your perception to a "4" Earth reality, which is one of survival and hope.

Reality is ever branching, you can always change the future. In fact, since you create the reality of the future, then, create a positive one. It is that simple.

I realize this is an unwordable concept. Words have not been invented yet in your languages which encompass this concept; when the concept becomes real to you human beings, you will then have words which describe it. Until then, I have done the best I (and this channel Diane), can do.

With all good blessings, I AM **R'Lu Xon**

CHAPTER TWENTY-THREE:
WARNING REGARDING THE HAARP PROJECT
AND THE POLAR ICE SHELVES

First a quick recap of what the U.S. "Haarp Project" is:

It is housed at a top secret facility in central Alaska. There are 36 antenna which form the visible part of a powerful and sophisticated high frequency radio transmitter designed to transform areas of the upper atmosphere into the equivalent of huge lenses, mirrors, and antennas. This is radio-physics at its most advanced. The research is Pentagon-sponsored.

There are objectives such as:

*Injecting high frequency radio waves into the ionosphere to create huge, extremely low frequency (ELF) virtual antennas used for earth-penetrating tomography. That is, peering deep inside the surface of the Earth.

*Heating regions of the upper and lower ionosphere to form virtual "lenses" and "mirrors" that can reflect a broad range of radio frequencies over the horizon to detect cruise missiles and - whatever.

*Generating ELF radio waves in the ionosphere to communicate across large distances with submarines.

*Creating a "full global shield" that would destroy ballistic missiles (or whatever), by overheating their electric guidance systems as they fly through the powerful radio energy field.

*Manipulating local weather

This is Veritan. I come to you in the light of logic.

We now need your energies in this matter, my enlightened human friend, to insure that this project does not materialize to the fullest potential. Allow me to briefly give our objections to each of the "goals" mentioned above:

* Penetrating the Earth at a deep level with ELF waves will wreck havoc with ecological and dimensional fields which emanate from deep inside Gaia. This penetration is a rape. It will turn reality topsy turvy, interrupting the most delicate and precious "inner workings" of the planet.

* Just read the words of the second objective! To "heat regions of the upper and lower ionosphere, creating lenses and mirrors.

Do they have any intelligence at all? Anyone can perceive what the creation of huge "mirrors" would do to an already over-heated planet, suffering from global warming. This planet's ice caps are melting faster than anyone had anticipated.

* ELF waves bombarding the land and atmosphere are very dangerous to life! This is the goal so as to communicate with submarines? Their submarines will have no life on the planet to "defend" if they play around with ELF waves and a super-heated ionosphere.

* The global shield they speak of, will keep positive aliens from helping the people and life forms of Earth. It is our electronic guidance systems they hope to upset. More crashed saucers give them even more advanced technology they should not and must not have. They hope to either capture us or make us go away as a self-defense measure.

* Controlling the weather - need I even comment?

I have voiced only a few of the major concerns we have and which any intelligence individual would have. You need not be a scientist to comprehend this.

We ask your help, a spiritual energy in-put toward raising the frequency entirely so that projects such as this simply die out, because they will exist in an extinct dimension.

Now I would like to speak on a different but related subject, the melting of the Antarctic's ice shelves (this general crisis also applies to the Arctic ice cap).

Glaciologists the world over agree that the Antarctic ice shelves are melting at an alarming rate. You might say, "But last winter was one of the coldest on record, so doesn't that add to the ice again?" No, sadly, it does not. Global warming is making the climate more extreme, but the movement is toward warming. It is simply that there is more moisture in the atmosphere (the greenhouse effect), thus there are more blizzards, ice, and winter conditions.   Major parts of the Larsen Ice

Shelf along the east side of the Antarctic have melted. Gone is that stretch of the shelf which connected James Ross Island with the Antarctic Peninsula.

Farther south, an iceberg half the size of Prince Edward Island has broken away from the Larsen shelf and is now cruising southern oceans. In short, a continent which has been frozen for 20 million years is undergoing a persistent rise in temperature.

You might wonder how a rise in spiritual frequency can help this crisis. There are a number of ways. For one thing, once we can meet openly, face to face, with human beings and work with you, we can help you adjust to the change in climate. Our technology is very advanced. We cannot come into the open as long as governments are so hostile to us, but a point will come which we call The Change Point when they no longer rule or dictate.

Second, what is coming up is a dimensional change, so that in a way, you will not exist in the same world as you do now. This is very difficult to word, because the above paragraph also holds true. But you will live in a dimension which has increased spiritual/psychic impact and potential, so that you can then change reality (the climate, the weather) more easily with mind power.

In summation, the changing dimensional energy which stretches into the Healing Millennium, will give you a breathing space from the global warming crisis so that we can all re-group and create a permanent higher dimension and frequency.

We can all rise above the disaster, landing you in an alternate, positive Earth.

That is the goal, but there are steps to this goal along the way, some of which occur after The Change Point. However, being able to come out in the open and work with humans will be a moment of great celebration, even for the logical amongst us, like me.

If you feel great worry about all the bad things happening, just remember that there is a valid and workable answer to all the current crisis; raise the frequency, creating an Earth which flourishes in the new millennium.

This is **Veritan**, ending transmission.

CHAPTER TWENTY-FOUR:
LOW SPERM COUNT/OVER-POPULATION PARADOX

This is Micha. I come to you in unconditional love.

Those of you who read Diane Tessman's publications regularly will know me well. I have worked with her **Star Network** since its inception. I am Tibus' best friend, having gone through time and space at his side, perhaps forever.

This is a fact for particular celebration because Tibus' home source is that of the future human consciousness, while my home source is a far distant planet. Yet and still, we remain brothers.

I am a healer but I have medical expertise as well. I heal my patients with spiritual and psychic energy, but I also heal with my scientific, medical knowledge.

As the light dawns on the Healing Millennium, you will find that the arts of healing and medical science go hand in hand. There is no real contradiction, simply two paths leading to the same goal: Healing the patient.

The patient has the best chance if both are applied. However, both must be used with intelligence.

There is much about medical science as the Dark Millennium closes, that is not intelligent. Strong drugs and surgery are much over-used. Monetary profit is entirely too important to the medical industry. To put it in a cynical manner, cancer and other ailments are big money to medical corporations.

However, an ill individual should not depend on a spiritual healer of low expertise and/or no talent, to cure ailments. Just because an individual says he or she is a "spiritual healer," it does not make it so. Know your healer well.

A wondrous helpmate to both spiritual and medical healing is the use of herbs. The Mother Planet has literally created an herb to heal every affliction known to Man and Animal.

Herbalism is an exciting field of knowledge to pursue, and I urge you to do so, especially at this crucial time in your planet's Change Times. The circle is ever revolving and herbalism is once again very important to humankind.

The Change Times is a time full of paradoxes; this curious phenomenon of paradox is always present as a planet goes through its time of great evolution.

We know that human over-population is one of the gravest threats to the planet. There are simply not enough resources to go around, nor enough space.

Humankind is at this point, a negative, parasitic infestation on the surface of Gaia. Still, population growth especially in the Third World, continues to mushroom at an incredible rate. We address this specific subject in **Earth Changes Bible.**

What I want to address myself to in this transmission, is the paradox which is also occurring. Recently it has become known by leading Earth scientists through extensive research, that the human race is on the road to extinction. Why? Because human males as of the year 1996 had half the sperm count their fathers did. If this trend continues, human males will be sterile, or virtually sterile, in a generation.

Between the lessening sperm count, the HIV virus, and other new and terrible mutating viruses, the human race is in serious trouble (danger of extinction), if it continues in the present dimension.

Why is the human male sperm count decreasing so dramatically? It is partially due to human males being exposed to chemicals. Five hundred measurable chemicals have been added to the human body since 1920.

For instance, plastics are very harmful to sperm creation in males. We of Space/Time Intelligence do not use plastics at all for a number of good reasons.

Also, the ozone situation is hard on male sperm creation as well as other contaminations of the environment, caused by humans themselves. The ozone influence on human sperm count will be discovered and highlighted more in the future.

Right now, the blame is mostly placed on chemicals. They have certainly done their share! Most of the research on the decrease in the human sperm count was done with males from the Developed World.

So, you might ask if Third World males have the same problem? They do to a large extent, although they are not as exposed to plastics, for instance. But most are out in the sun (ozone exposure), and there are, sadly, many new viruses taking a grasp on the Third World.

So, yes, the problem is also there. This is a species problem.

The question might well be, will the human male sperm count go low enough to stop the population explosion soon enough to save the planet from the infestation of humans?

This is what Gaia hopes. And, herein lies the bottom line truth of why human sperm count is decreasing at an alarming rate: The Mother Planet has decreed it in an effort to control her wayward child.

Tragically, the same components which are killing humanity are also killing The Mother Planet. In a sense, this is fitting, since the two are linked so totally.

It is Gaia's hope, however, that she can get humankind under control before her own death is imminent. It is the law of nature to eliminate a species when that species becomes completely out of balance with the rest of its world.

Humankind has caused the imbalance.

Humankind may well be eliminated by the imbalance.

That sounds cruel, but it is the way of the cosmos.

"What goes around, comes around."

"Do unto others as you would have them do unto you."

However, just as we believe Mother Earth is a planet worth saving, we also believe the human race is a species worth saving.

We believe that The Creator Spirit gave us, the Space/Dimensional Intelligence, our many blessings in order to help others. So, this is also how The Creator works, and we are now trying our hardest to save both Earth and humanity.

God, The Creator, works through the intelligence of individuals, and in fact is the intelligence of individuals.

The potential of Earth and humanity is so great!

Again, we concede that the situation cannot go on as it is. So, we do wish to show humanity that a new, shining world exists where you can do it right this time! All that is needed is a higher spiritual frequency than what exists on Earth.

Remember, this higher frequency will happen in the Healing Millennium. That is the miracle and the promise. It is up to each of you to raise your consciousness enough to join the future.

As to the specific problem of the sterility of the human male:

Obviously if this does happen (if things keep going as they are), there are ways to solve this problem in order to keep the race going in some meager way.

This would be rather like keeping the tiger's species alive by maintaining one hundred tigers in zoos rather than thousands in the wild, as Nature intended.

Measures which can be taken for the human race are very restrictive and un-natural. Females could basically be cloned from female eggs; this has already happened on a sheep research farm in Scotland.

Indeed, some of our alien friends come from races which lost the ability to reproduce naturally millennia ago, and have turned to a process similar to cloning and other scientific measures.

We do not allow cloning, just as Tibus has explained. But in order to keep an entire species from extinction, we do occasionally allow a similar process.

However, clones are never created for the many reasons which are "handy" for other individuals. And in fact, the process of creating life from the female egg, is not technically cloning. Still, we keep very restrictive perimeters on this process.

The genetic vigor of a species is more precious than the human race has possibly realized, because you have been genetically and reproductively vigorous until now. You as a race do not realize what a gift this is, until you lose it.

We do not see the desperation measures similar to cloning, as becoming a necessary practice for humanity. Even the researchers who discovered the trend toward very low human sperm counts, have optimism that this trend toward species sterility can be reversed. The problem with that is, the population explosion will then continue marching along, gobbling up the entire planet. In fact, it is marching along at an alarming rate even now, despite lowering sperm counts.

If we can accomplish a risen frequency, this low sperm count problem is eliminated, as well as the problem of the population explosion. It is a sad fact that not all human beings are enlightened enough to make it into the future reality; this is a sad but realistic answer to the problem of "too many people."

Sperm counts will rise because the vigor of the race will be renewed as the consciousness ascension takes place.

Is it terrible to admit that many people will die because they cannot raise their frequency sufficiently to live in the new dimension? We remind you that they simply will not be able to live in a frequency which is alien to theirs; this would be like a fish trying to live on land, or like trying to plug in an electrical appliance which runs on 110 voltage, into a 220 socket.

It is difficult to explain in detail, but these people will not literally "die," they will simply fade into the oblivion of the past.

The frequency of the individual must connect to the frequency of the dimension. And it is the choice of each individual, whether to become enlightened or remain stagnant, until the lights go out.

It does not matter if he or she dwells in a backward culture or a modern one, each individual has the choice to be of good intent, wherever he dwells. It is basically this simple choice which will see him (or her) through to the Healing Millennium. People of "backward" cultures will be able to adjust to the Healing Millennium as well as people from more modern cultures.

The coming spiritual cleansing will also be a physical one. The chemicals, plastics, contaminants, radiation, and so forth, will be cleansed and removed in order that the race start anew.

Cancer is becoming common because of the need for human spiritual cleansing. Cancer begins to increase when any race begins its genetic decline, but especially if there are escalating environmental crisis. Cancer is a universal medical phenomenon in races which are struggling to climb the awareness ladder or perish. It is a self- destruct mechanism on a species-wide basis.

Its increase is, in other words, a sign of The Change Times. Cancer can be fought and conquered on a spiritual, psychic basis. Of this there is no doubt.

Raising the consciousness into a new dimension, cleanses the species' physical vessel. Time and time again, we perceive that the best answer to a number of current crisis is to raise the frequency! Often it is the only answer.

I send my blessings and guidance. Contact us, we are here for you, enlightened ones.

Micha

Vision of the New Age

Artist: Carol Ann Rodriguez

CHAPTER TWENTY-FIVE:
THE TRUE NEW AGE, AND THE FAKE NEW AGE

This is Celiera. I come to you with the sureness and power of the river's current.

How long ago was it I first sent a transmission your way, Diane? Was it 1986 or 1987? Certainly some of your years have passed since first you were introduced to me. I am the Spirit of the River, a nature entity to be sure.

My consciousness is also with the Space/Time Intelligence to which Tibus and other friends belong. I, too, am trying to help save this magnificent planet which is my native home. I give thanks to my alien friends who do not spring from Gaia's bosom, who nonetheless, are working very hard to save her.

How can a nature spirit be a cognizant member of an advanced intelligence which uses UFOs and other high technology? I am billions of years old, just as the Mother Planet is. In that time, I have evolved to a higher awareness which you might call my Whole Self, or Higher Self. The Seven Rays of Consciousness shone like a rainbow upon my waters, and I evolved.

You can still perceive me as the Spirit of the River when you gaze at a stream or river; the early Celts embraced the concept that each river has a living spirit with whom you can communicate. They also worshipped the spirits of specific rivers. They were a very wise tribe in a number of ways.

My Higher Self has become, throughout many aeons, a consciousness (a presence) who can contribute much to groups such as my friends of Space/Time Intelligence. No, I am not aboard a starship pressing computer buttons, I am not that kind of physical being. But I do have a higher intelligence and I do indeed love my Mother Planet dearly. I hope beyond hope that we can save her.

Humans must begin to realize that the Space/Time Intelligence are not simply "aliens from another planet." Our group is not even "aliens from another planet, inter-dimensional Earth beings, plus angels of higher realms." These descriptions of us only touch on who and what we are.

What is happening to Earth is an enormous event; for the first time, realms are opening which you have only dreamed of, and there are many realms you have not possibly dreamed of. But soon, you will perceive much more!

The term "Gaia" is used to indicate the living spirit of the Mother Planet; it emphasizes that she is alive just as you are.

The human race has the ability to bastardize just about anything, and this is a subject on which I wish to communicate:

We are concerned that the dawning human awareness about Gaia will become corrupted by people "jumping on the bandwagon" to make a profit.

Also, governments are jumping aboard, in order to diffuse a powerful movement which is ultimately stronger than they are. That movement is Man returning spiritually to his Mother Planet and thus to the beings and energies of the cosmos.

Allow me to give an example of a misuse of this precious dawning awareness:

There are shops called "earth stores." They have beautifully polished, very ornate crystals, rocks, all sorts of natural items presented in a fancier manner than the gemstone trader at your local flea market can ever accomplish. These chain stores belonging to large corporations exist for reasons of large profit only.

The gemstone trader at your local flea market may sell geodes which are being plundered from Mother Earth. Geodes have been dug up for years now, often in a method similar to strip mining, but not nearly as large an operation.

However, the "dent" in Mother Earth which small gemstone traders make, is minuscule. It is rather like a fisherman setting out in a small canoe, and eventually spearing one endangered turtle.

But, the big, slick "earth shops" which exist in large, expensive shopping malls, insist their geodes (and similar items from Mother Earth), must be perfect, unlike the flea market geodes. They sell these geodes for a lot of money.

How much earth was torn up to render one perfect "Earth store" specimen? It would be like wiping out a herd of endangered turtles to get one perfect specimen.

And what about the coffee mugs with grand pictures of the highly endangered Tiger at these charming, slick, stores? There may be a sign which says, "Some proceeds go to help the world's wildlife." How much of the proceeds? Upon research you may find it is one half of one percent. Yet, highly aware, well meaning people buy a coffee mug feeling they have also helped Gaia.

These people would have helped much more to simply give a donation to their favorite ecology, wildlife, or animal rights charity. Now, some conspiracy buffs will say that even respected environmental groups are run by the "New World Order." This is where conspiracy paranoia goes amok and does damage.

You must believe in something! And, you should help in active ways as well as spiritual ways. Do not let the handy paranoid conspiracy theories make you immobile and stagnant in your efforts to help. Look into your heart and soul, and if your guidance is that your contribution is going to truly help, then please do make your donation. Our guidance is that most of the environmental, wildlife, and animal welfare groups are true in intent and usually do apply money well.

But do stay on top of this situation. It is possible in the future that some of these groups will be taken over (or an attempt will be made), by this New World Order of multinational corporations who plan to cash in on humankind's rising awareness of "Gaia."

Their ultimate plan would be to get control of the "renegade" people of high spiritual awareness. They reason, "If you can't beat' em, join 'em."

The thrust of this transmission, my friends, is to beg you to be discerning regarding "earth" and "New Age" products, services, and practitioners.

Do you perceive how the people of Earth, just as they are about to gain beautiful higher awareness, might be tricked? Just as you begin to care, this caring will be taken advantage of to make money by a few greedy individuals who haven't a hope of evolving spiritually! Do not let yourself be sabotaged.

The way to avoid this is for you, the enlightened person, to be smarter than the corporations think you are. Do not fall for sleek packaging or trendy stuff. Use your logic and intellect. Then, look to your intuition, look into your heart, in order to know what is pure and true.

If a supposed New Age company or individual has the money for a mass mailing to millions of people, promoting expensively produced material, just where is the source of his or her money? Is the packaging prettier than the content? Does it show true knowledge of metaphysics? Is it intelligent or is there an annoying illogic to the whole thing? Is one individual's "ego" very evident in the material? Is his or her product so wonderful that millions of dollars have already been made, then re-invested? That is the impression they will try to give you. You will find most New Age companies have not been around that long.

It is more likely that the company has bank funding from a large corporation or cartel which is dying to take your money, make a profit, and which could care less about true New Age ideas. In fact, to divert money and energy from the true New Age concepts may be the ultimate goal.

So think and feel twice before you fall for the bright, slick colors of expensive packaging. The concern I express at this time is that "Gaia" and New Age concepts may become totally misused by multinational corporations in order to abort the enlightenment movement, make a huge profit for themselves, and gain power and control over the people of Earth, right as you are about to liberate yourselves.

Be true to yourself! Don't be impressed by "perfect" or "polished." Stick to what is truly of Gaia and of her sacred energy. You, my enlightened friend, have the ability to distinguish!

Don't buy the perfect polished geode at the mall shop for $300.00. Go down to the river and pick up that "dirty but sort of pink" rock which has caught your eye from time to time; wash it off, feel and work with its unique energy. Use it for meditation. Don't fall for every Hollywood film which comes down the turnpike, don't buy every dinosaur t-shirt from a huge corporation's theme shop in a huge corporation's theme park. I know, life is short and it is hard to be so idealistic every moment. Sometimes there must be a bit of fun.

This is why rivers have rapids and do not just roll along lazily mile after mile. But, would it not be as much fun to buy a handmade vest, sold at your local flea market by an earthy woman who loves to talk about UFOs and higher awareness, as to buy the expensive, trendy dinosaur t-shirt with the Hollywood studio logo on it? We urge you, do not throw the baby out with the bath water!

You must continue your communication with Gaia, your protection of her, your cleansing/healing love of her. This is what is pure, real, and true. It has nothing to do with multinational corporations or schemes.

You must know the real spirit of Gaia so intimately, that you will not fall for fancy, expensive, slickly packaged schemes.

Go ahead, create your new reality in the Healing Millennium, my human friend. We will help you. All reality is created by you. Make it better!

Celiera, the Spirit of the River

CHAPTER TWENTY-SIX:
POTENTIAL MASS INSANITY

This is Tibus. I come to you in love and light.

I am channeling this to Diane in the early morning, and it seems to me that the term "raising the frequency" might once in a while get stale; so I would like to refer to it in another way. A very clear way of explaining a "new dimension" is simply to say, "It is a new day." This bright morning is not yesterday, it is a new day, after crossing a field (a period) of darkness. In The Healing Millennium, you will not be in "yesterday" any longer.

Reaching a new dimension of higher frequency is as easy as waking up to the new day. This I promise you. The act of changing dimensions, even if caused by a polar shift in the magnetism of the planet, is in itself not a difficult one for those who are spiritually aware and ready for it.

It is, however, most helpful to know what is happening and why.

This is why we fear mental illness and even death for those of lower awareness who don't know what's happening and who will not be able to adapt.

This is why, as the Twentieth Century closes, there are so many unthinkable crimes, from serial killings to bizarre crimes of sexual nature to deadly terrorism. This is why a young generation has turned so tragically to heavy drugs, to keep themselves numb. Every consciousness can sense that the base of reality is unraveling. This sends panic, fear, and trauma rippling through the mass consciousness; these horrific vibrations manifest for those who are still totally tuned to the old lower frequency where this unraveling is acutely felt. They react in negative ways, it is a mass insanity.

For those who feel the unraveling but reach upward and work toward raising their consciousness, the negative reactions do not occur. Still, you know logically that things are unraveling!

I promise you that our new dimension can and will come, as easily as the sun rises on a new day. The new day begins with the the Healing Millennium's birth. Just as with a new day, your world will at first seem the same. Your animal friends will be with you, Mother Nature will be bursting with energy outside your door.

But it will soon become clear to your perception that this is a brand new day, a brand new dimension. The frequency will have risen. It will not happen just as the clock strikes on New Year in 2000 or 2001; but, soon afterward, the mass consciousness of the new millennium will become established in the fabric of reality, as the mind of God turns toward a new day.

Now I would like to discuss another matter which also poses a "mass insanity" threat: Negative aliens have given governments and militaries many high tech secrets which they should not have shared.

These include secrets in the field of pschotronics. Psitronics (also called psychotronics), puts together advanced technology with "psychic waves," which are the subatomic waves and particles which are the "habitats" of consciousness.

This field of advanced science is almost always used negatively, to control minds. It can be used to control the minds of billions, or of one. A "machine" can send out psi waves and convince the enemy's army that they are all dead. This would be their reality. Indeed, they would be dead, through the power of suggestion. No weapon would have to be used, no risk taken by the other side.

This is but one of an endless number of evil uses for this field of technology. The HAARP Project, mentioned previously, also has psitronic aspects.

We of Space/Time Intelligence are trying to get this research under control and thrown out the proverbial door. But we must ask ourselves, what short of mind control can we use to prevent mind control devices?

We ourselves would have to battle to keep our accurate view of reality and alternate realities, if psiwaves were aimed at us, carrying images of false realities. You, my friends, would have to struggle very hard also.

This would seem like a bout with something similar to paranoia or schizophrenia. We are confident that you as an enlightened being would prevail.

We also know we would, because of our high spiritual awareness and knowledge of "things psychic." This is why you would win also.   To consciously know what is happening, is half the battle! The goodness and enlightenment of your soul is the other half of the battle against evil.

We fear for the masses of unenlightened minds across the globe who do not know what is happening and are not growing spiritually.   To   conclude   this transmission on a more inspiring note, I wish to give you the following stream of consciousness to consider: Isn't "time" something of an illusion? The future always lies before us, an open door and a blank slate.

Of course one action leads to another, one step leads to the next, so in that sense, the future is somewhat outlined. However, even taking that into account, the future still hinges on spontaneous acts and events to a huge degree.

As I have traveled the universe, of one thing I have become sure:

Consciousness is much more real than "time."

Consciousness is much more powerful than "time."

Metaphysics tells us that "time" doesn't even exist. I have also heard the metaphysical statement that "time is death."

If you could step outside of "time," would you beat death?

Where would you be if you were at a point in the fabric of space, without the dimension of "time?" Would you have left your old human identity behind and have become a "super being?"

Would you have become a cosmic citizen?

One version of the Change Point, my friends, is that "time" itself has indeed run out at that point.

But, life survives.

Consciousness survives. And flourishes, unshackled by the false illusion of "time."

Quantum physics tells us that intersect points in time occur simultaneously, but at this point in your development, you only perceive these points as linear so that your consciousness can give order to all your experiences.

At present, your consciousness can only focus on one experience at a time, so your focus (perception) keeps changing, giving the illusion of time.

If you can learn to control that focus rather than it controlling you (thus giving you the illusion of time), then you have beat "time." You have emerged into cosmic citizenship.

You have become your Whole Self.

Our perception "out here" focuses on all our experiences, all our lifetimes.

But, I do not aim to make it sound so difficult to achieve, as if you need to rub your head and scratch your stomach at the same time.

The new day which is about to dawn is a day which has all these perceptions in it. This is its "hum," its vibration. It will be easy for you to join it.

The only impossible thing to do if you are to survive, is to stay stagnant at the old low frequency.

May the healing light of goodness surround you, always,
Tibus

CHAPTER TWENTY-SEVEN:
WHAT ABOUT THE CHILDREN?

This is Tibus. I come to you in love and light.

As any dimension unravels, the young ones of that dimension suffer the most. Children need social structure. They need to be close to Mother Nature. They need to be close to their family. They need these aspects of their environment now more than ever, and it is now when they are least available.

In the current world as the Dark Millennium ebbs away, society has come undone. It is at this time that such monsters as child pornography and child abuse are more likely to happen in greater numbers.

Mother Nature has been destroyed in many places around the world so that children cannot know and touch her. Concrete jungles are all they know. It is almost impossible for a child to know the God Spark within if he or she does not know Mother Nature. Millions of families have been forced to leave farms or small acreages as big corporations take over the farms. Small town lifestyles have been destroyed as factories close.

In so many ways, children of the late Twentieth Century are denied access to their Mother Planet and her nurturing energies. They have been denied a secure family situation as well. They in turn become insensitive with a, "Who cares?" attitude. The Family, as it once was, has become nearly extinct. Of course the lack of a loving family structure can hurt the child badly.

A phenomenon which is a "by-product" of the unraveling of dimensional energies is the drastic rise in the number of children who are autistic.

These little souls are sometimes tuned into a totally different reality than the one which exists in the daily world. Others are truly confused on a consciousness level, not being able to "home in" on the weak, fading frequency of the daily world around them but not able to find another "home frequency" either.

Many children find their parents working long hours hoping to make financial ends meet. Do not let your leaders tell you how good things are in the nation. The majority of citizens are financially poorer than ever before; millions of individuals who were "middle class" now find themselves struggling in the lower financial class. A few super wealthy individuals get richer and richer.

The frequencies of the Seven Rays of Consciousness need to be raised for our children and for our children's children, most of all!

I, Tibus, am your children's children's child, so again I reassure you that there is great hope, promise, and potential for a positive new dawn, just ahead.

This new day will not come about in the dimension in which you live (remembering our knowledge on multiple branch realities), if you do not make it so.

I tell Diane that she did not teach first and second grades, and English as a Second Language, just to pass eleven years of her life. It is important to have enlightened individuals also experienced as teachers of children.

Sometimes Diane dreams that she is still teaching in the classroom and asks me why these dreams are so frequent. My answer, "To keep you sharp."

We do not mean literally going back to the classroom because the present educational system is antiquated and will not survive the Change Times. A new educational approach must be developed.

Obviously most human children would feel more at home with an enlightened human teacher than a well meaning alien. This, then, is a vital part of many of your missions, my enlightened friends. Some of you will be involved in helping children bridge the gap between the old and new dimensions, between the dark past and the bright future. For some, this will be an on-going mission if you so choose it to be. Some children presently on Earth, are souls who came to help in these Change Times, and they will adjust more quickly than anyone to the risen frequency. We encourage you, our enlightened friends, to write children's stories at this time or to do other similar creating which reflects your high frequency; this frequency will reach the children through your creations and help them survive and flourish.

Some readers have grandchildren; a wise, enlightened, loving grandparent is one of the most precious friends a child can have, especially in these crisis times.

If a child you know has invisible playmates or displays other spiritual or psychic gifts, help this child especially to reach for the positive as he or she experiences contact with "The Great Unknown." Let him or her know how wonderful it is to be blessed with spiritual talents; there is no more precious gift, especially now.

A species is doomed if it cannot give its best to its children.

Often these days, the human race gives its worst to its children.

However, there is still great hope, and within the children, there is unlimited potential!

With enlightened humans and spiritual guardians to guide them, the children of Earth will become evolved Future Humans. They will be just as wonderfully, and unpredictably "human" as their ancestors, but theirs will be the first generation to celebrate and embrace their God-given right to cosmic citizenship!

May the healing light of goodness surround you, always,

Tibus

ADDITIONAL RELATED THOUGHTS FROM DIANE AND TIBUS

We always encourage people to be active in environmental causes or whatever physical cause feels right; any physical activism in which you are involved because you are concerned and caring, is also food for your spirit.

However, "spiritual activism" is something a bit different; you must take an aggressive role in practicing spiritual/psychic endeavors which you know can create and shape a better reality.

Diane was watching the feature film on **Nostradamus** recently and it occurred to her that he was very much a spiritual warrior (spiritual activist).

Nostradamus was aggressive all his life in putting forth his beliefs and visions; it seemed he really could not hide his amazing gift and did not want to. And, he nearly got killed for it many times.

Organized Christianity did a good job of making most people afraid to be openly metaphysical, psychic, or mystical, and this fear still hangs over us today.

Many of us have past life memories of being burned at the stake or tortured to death during The Inquisition. Our contact Veritan apparently also experienced this in a human lifetime, and so did many other guardians in the higher realms.

Also, many of us have hurtful memories from this lifetime of facing pressure from organized religion or non-understanding peers, acquaintances, or family members.

It is terribly sad that one of the greatest God-given gifts, the psychic ability, is considered to be "from the dark side." How did this ever happen? We know how it happened throughout history, but how could humanity let it happen?

In fact, the psychic ability allows the God Spark to shine through from within, as few other gifts do; in the same wonderful category might be the God-given voice of an opera singer or the dancing ability of a ballet star.

Many of our **Star Network** friends have explained that they used to be shy, hiding their spiritual and psychic gifts. But now, sometimes despite pressure from family members or society, they simply must let these gifts shine without apology.

Diane has had the experience of having to make herself "shine," during New Age conferences and other public appearances, because one's first instinct, no matter where you are, is to hide your "alien quality." This is a self-protective measure developed early in childhood.

We must know in these final years of the Dark Millennium, beyond a shadow of a doubt, that an enlightened, spiritual nature is a gift to be proud of. It is not only necessary in these difficult days, but your enlightenment may well save the entire world.

Let your light shine, be a spiritual warrior!

This message comes from Tibus, with love and light, as well as from Diane.

Diane in front of Ft. Severson, first Norwegian settlement in Mitchell County, IA. The fort is rumored to be haunted.

CHAPTER TWENTY-EIGHT:
CROP CIRCLE REVELATIONS

This is Oniocole of The Tuatha De Danann.

Diane, you have not heard from an individual within The Tuatha De Danann before; always before you have heard from "The Family of Diane" as one voice. This is because we are a group soul to some degree, evolved beyond the level at which humanity has arrived in the late 20th Century. We do not have the petty squabbles and prejudices which you do, and we share telepathic ability. We are therefore united as one telepathic voice, but individuals of us may "speak" if we wish. The cruelties and greediness of humankind drove us from the surface of Celtic Ireland long ago. We had settled there after arriving from the sky in very ancient times.

Throughout these several millennia that we have been "sideways to the sun," we have continued to develop mentally, physically, emotionally, and spiritually, in our own dimension. We have moved closer to becoming a "one soul" vibration. However, we take great pleasure and pride in also functioning as individual beings. Many of us are downright eccentric individuals.

We have decided it is time to give you more details on the "crop circle" phenomenon; I am something of an expert on this surface phenomenon, so I am honored to be the first of The Tuatha De Danann to channel individually to you.

When I say, "I am something of an expert on crop circles," I could also say, "I am a specialist in creating crop circles."

Yes, I create some of them and, yes, I appear as a glowing orb of translucent light when I am at work. In a sense, I don't want to remove the mystery for you about "crop circles" because mystical mysteries are a wonderful, vibrant part of life itself. The question is truly as thrilling as the answer!

However, it is time we ourselves turned a bit more toward "the sun" of perception and recognition (of our existence) and surrendered our secure "sideways to the sun" dimensional stance. We will soon have little choice in this matter, as explained in the channeling by Tibus in his transmission on Inner Earth Dwellers.

So, what are your questions?

First, why are some crop circles more ornate than others?

Because, just as with channeling, our ability to "deliver" psychic messages upon the surface of the Earth varies; I will liken this to a first grader learning to print to a senior in high school jotting down intricate notes in well-practiced longhand (script). We who dwell primarily under in the Celtic Isles and who manifest on that ancient surface from time to time, have been perceived and recognized over the years by the native humans of the Celtic Isles. They call us "fairies."

However, those of us who dwell under Ohio (as an example), were perceived and recognized by the Native Americans only. Tragically, the Native Americans were nearly decimated in numbers and influence. Especially hard hit was their Natural Belief System (religion) which included us.

Recently, however, we other-dimensional sub-surface beings have been perceived and recognized by star people and enlightened New Agers, even in Ohio and similar areas of the New World. Therefore, "first grade" simple crop circles can begin manifesting; this will be true elsewhere in America, too, as you learn to perceive us and recognize our consciousness. My cousins in the New World will become more skilled at crop circle creating, too.

The crop circles in our ancient lands of Ireland, Scotland, and Britain, are indeed more complex. But, you see, we have been perceived there for a much longer, and much steadier period. And so, we have a lot of experience at creating our works of art.

I should explain that we other-dimensional, sub-surface dwellers can travel very quickly, in your terms, to areas far across the planet. Basically, we reside "under" one area. This is much like you, is it not? The only difference is that we can travel in a matter of seconds, across the globe. This is because we are "light forms" as well as "life forms."

I must note three other items here:

The vast majority of we other-dimensional, sub-surface dwellers are very much of The Light. We are of the light side of The Force, so to speak, so do not think because we are "underneath," that we are negative. Also, I do acknowledge that there have been crop circle hoaxes by human beings for whatever silly purposes. I am not taking "credit" for any of their designs!

Our designs are very urgent, symbolic, and individualized, and we are very proud of them.

And a final note: While UFOs (nuts and bolts machines), have been known to create crop circles, the vast majority are created by us, with our unique psychic light power. In a sense, we are a force of Gaia herself.

You may be asking, "What do our crop circle messages mean?"

Our crop circle messages are works of art and particular to each artist (each specialist). However, our message is a "one voice" message. Symbolically, with signs and synchronicities within our circles, we hope to urgently communicate to humankind all of which this book speaks: Humankind is killing our mother, Planet Earth. Humankind must learn again to perceive and love Gaia, and to heal her after the damage done to her and her life forms. Humankind must, at this micro-second in history, evolve spiritually to the next step, which is cosmic citizenship, or perish. We create our circles to beg you to realize there are other forms of intelligence who also live in, under, and above this beautiful planet, and who are very worried about their own survival, "thanks" to humankind. This is our home too!

I need not spell it further for you, my enlightened friend, but I (we) do need to spell it out to the majority of humankind, and this is what we are doing!

To help us create more crop circles, you have merely to recognize our existence and attempt to perceive us when you are out in nature.

These days, we welcome communication from you, and even encounters. It was not always this way.

Just as the Native Americans and the Celt people believe in our existence, so must you. This is all we need to create more crop circles; you must help us manifest in this way. Channeling is more exhausting than creating the most intricate of my creations, so I will rest now.

I AM Oniocole, I close with blessings of love and good fortune

In an Irish apple orchard, Diane took this fairy photo

CHAPTER TWENTY-NINE:
SHOULD THE DOG SHAKE THE FLEAS?

This is Tibus. I come to you in love and light.

Before I get to the crux of this transmission, I wish to give you very encouraging news! Perhaps you have already heard? The Earth's ozone layer is healthier than it has been for years! Several of the holes in it have shrunk considerably. Did your prayers and meditations, plus your constant positive spiritual in-put have something to do with creating this more positive reality? Yes!

In an alternate reality, the ozone gaps have not shrunk and they continue to head for a catastrophic "9" or "10" on the Reality Continuum. The Earth's immune system is virtually destroyed in these alternate realities.

However, in your reality, enlightened souls have managed to create a less catastrophic situation. Did we of Space/Dimensional Intelligence have something to do with patching the ozone hole, similar to patching a tire? Yes. But do you not see that "we" cannot be separated from "you?"

We are One.

Is there still a long way to go, not only regarding the ozone crisis but so many other crisis? Yes, there is, but this marked improvement in the ozone situation shows that we can do it! The improvement came about, in practical terms, because human beings stopped using the CFC's which have punched holes in the ozone layer, which is Gaia's immune system. Even industry cut back somewhat on CFC use, and individuals did as well.

Few individuals realize that the greatest damage was done to the ozone layer by nuclear testing; governments do not tell their people this. However, there have been fewer above ground nuclear tests in recent years, so this is helpful also.

From this we give you the following message of hope:

As we have told you, Gaia, the living spirit of Mother Earth, can revive and heal easier and more quickly than you might possibly imagine! Earth is a most dynamic lady, a living essence of extreme creative power with an enormous love of life and for life. So many sad facts manifest regarding the tragic state of Earth, and all may seem lost, but I absolutely promise you that Earth can and will recover at a miraculous rate, once practical ecological measures are taken to save her, and once she receives the active spiritual love which human beings have denied her these many long years.

I promise you that a Risen Frequency of thinking, feeling, and being, is just around the corner, not nearly as far away or inaccessible as you might feel. The Seven Rays of Human Consciousness will intensify and rise upward.

Now, to the crux of my message:

We have heard it said that humans should not try to stop Mother Earth's anger with their psychic/spiritual efforts to heal the planet and raise the frequency.

Like a dog shaking fleas, some people feel Planet Earth must choose how many and how strong her violent upheavals are to be; they feel it is wrong to try to "control" the number and severity.

Humankind is viewed as an infestation by the Mother Planet, and, some people feel, humans must take what is coming to you (every last one of you).

After hearing this expressed by individuals she respects, Diane asked me if indeed Mother Earth should be allowed to get as angry as possible; are attempts to quell or lessen her anger, wrong? My answer is, your (and our) attempts to calm and lessen Earth's anger are not wrong, and we/you should be making these efforts. And, we are! No one deludes him or herself that an extremely peaceful "1" on the Reality Continuum will occur at this point. There is and will be a Change Times.

The child (humankind) has been presented with a formidable lesson to learn.

The anger, hurt, and frustration that the Mother Planet feels will not be totally restrained or put off, for another day. That is, we are not trying to have her "hold it in" for another thousand or million years. But, to use an analogy, if a friend is very hurt and angry, and says she intends to kill her ex-husband who did this to her, do you say, "Sure, go ahead and kill him." No, you work with her to calm her anger so that she will not kill him, also essentially ending her own productive life.

You help her vent her justifiable anger and help her see that there is life for her after this very insensitive man has left her life. You show her that she has great potential. In the same way, if our star people can alleviate some of Earth's anger through communicating with her, and through simply loving her, so that an earthquake is a "6.5" instead of an "8.5" on the Richter Scale, should this work not be attempted?

Of course it should!

The improvement of the ozone situation involves a healing of the damage inflicted by humankind; certainly you should attempt to heal this damage! It would not be there if it were not for your race of beings.

You are not going against the cosmic flow, my enlightened friend, to work with Gaia and to try to create a less severe Change Times.

Certainly to just let Doomsday happen, is not within the cosmic flow. The Creator gave you a brain, spiritual power, and a strong will, and as such, you are within the cosmic flow to use these to influence a more positive reality for this magnificent blue/green world. In fact, you would be out of the cosmic flow and balance if you did not try to create a more positive outcome.

You are the hands of The Creator, you bring The Creator's will to the planet.

God/Goddess is within you and as such you have a cosmic responsibility to work for a more positive reality. Without **you**, full potential will not happen.

Keep your eye on the highest star. Do not become side-tracked with scenarios given you by negative influences. Do not become lost in your own emotional conflicts. We all have these, but the goal is much bigger and more urgent than this. Saving the planet and raising the frequency is what truly counts.

May the healing light of goodness surround you, always,

Tibus

CHAPTER THIRTY:
A PLEA FROM THE GUARDIAN OF THE OCEANS

This is the Guardian Spirit of the Oceans.

The ancients personified me into a god who had several names. My favorite was "Neptune." I never felt this "god" concept caught my true beinghood but it was a well-intentioned attempt by human beings. Because the ancients traveled the oceans and seas in vulnerable boats, they were highly aware of my power. They depended on my good nature in their fishing and traveling endeavors, and they greatly feared my bad moods.

The concept of The Sirens was also an interesting attempt by humankind, to personify me. Once in a while, I would "get myself together" and manifest a "siren" for a weary sailor. She would have long hair, be immensely beautiful, and sing a sad but irresistible tune, beckoning him. She/I did not always beckon his ship toward deadly rocks. Usually, I was just playing with him, just as my sea gulls did. I helped his boredom.

And my "mermaids" were another of my splendid manifestations! In these, I attempted to give humans a genetic split between their image (the human body) and one of mine (the fish). Yes, for millennia, it has been not only my billions of ocean creatures which inhabited my waters, it has been my spiritual and psychic manifestations as well. Make no mistake, these are real!

You may notice that I have put much in the past tense. This is because The Guardian of the Oceans (me), has grown weak. I am sick.

I do not feel like playing these days. My immunity is almost non-existent. My immunity reflects the weakened state of my Mother Planet's immune system. Could it be otherwise?

1998 is the International Year of the Oceans according to sixteen hundred scientists from sixty-five countries. I realize they are making an effort to draw attention to my plight, but, truly, this effort is not enough. It is too little too late. I am in real trouble. I have not spoken before because I preferred not to, but now I feel I must. My coral reefs are dying. Red tides wipe out sea creatures, billions at a time. The White Abalone is virtually gone. There are few Cod in New England waters.

El Nino demolishes shorelines and beaches, where my turtles nest. Waters are too warm for my sea lions, and 75% die as El Nino prevails. El Nino also has given a deadly boost to "hantavirus" which destroys both land and sea beings. One-celled killers are destroying my incredibly beautiful dolphins, manatees, and other sea mammals as well as many other ocean creatures.

Amphibians, those funny, wondrous half and half creatures, are declining at an alarming rate due to depletion of Earth's ozone layer; they are particularly vulnerable to radiation. This connects also to the demise of my coral reefs. All is connected! When one card topples, they all do!

The sad truth is, the list in endless. Each of you can easily add ten more ocean environmental tragedies to the list above. Humankind has dumped chemicals, radioactive substances, toxic medical waste, plastics, human waste, and many other pollutants, into Mother Earth's cherished oceans and seas.

This is sadly symbolic as well as realistically deadly. Humankind has polluted the very waters from which it came, the miraculous salty waters of creation! This is Earth's precious, sacred blood.

You have taken too much from me and you have put too much into me!

I must not let my current despair and depression be my final defeat, however. I must reach **you**, an individual of enlightenment, and explain the situation clearly to you (as clearly as sparkle my Caribbean waters); you must know that all is not lost, but that **you** are the one to save me!

You see, it is you who will bring a higher dimension to Earth. In this new reality, I will have the strength to renew myself. This is because the higher frequency will not only affect the human consciousness, it will affect Gaia's consciousness as well. Just as humankind will be renewed in a higher frequency, so will all of Earth. It is not only humanity's risen consciousness which must come about, it is also Earth's.

Gaia, the living spirit of Earth, is also about to take a step upward in spiritual evolution. With this step comes healing energy, rejuvenation, a new "lease on life." It makes perfect sense, does it not? Humankind and Mother Earth are inescapably bound; humankind is Earth's child. The two must rise together!

You know, my enlightened friend, that we have a "catch 22" occurring here, because you must help manifest the risen frequency, and yet, the risen frequency will give you and all life forms on Earth, renewed life and energy with which to make the leap.

The rise in spiritual frequency will give you and all of us spirits on Earth, a life free of chemical contaminants, nuclear leaks, and toxic wastes; we will also be gloriously free of the greed which has caused our severe problems in the first place. The same greed in power hungry individuals which harms your life, is the greed which has depleted my waters of the fish which were once so abundant.

You and I have the same enemies, the same goals, the same hopes.

You have only to do two things: One: Please carry us through to the New Dawn. We Nature Spirits cannot do this, the ball is not in our court. The ball is in the human court; this is your move, Humanity. This is your Time of Learning and Growing. (It is you who have caused the damage).

Second, my enlightened human friends must participate in spiritual cleansing and healing efforts which emphasize healing the illness of the oceans and seas in particular. You must do this now, as the new millennium draws near.

You can accomplish this through prayer, meditation, or simply by being close to nature and feeling good thoughts. Walk in Earth's forests, prairies, and along her ocean shores. Really listen to what she is telling you. Get into real contact with her consciousness! Truly offer her your love and healing energies.

Of course you must also be as involved in environmental efforts as your time and financial situation permit. Become involved in local environmental concerns. The Physical and The Spiritual go hand in hand, they are two halves of The Whole.

It is fortunate that the ley energies of Mother Earth, which correspond to your chakra system, have increased in their natural cycle at present, or spirits such as I would really be lost.

As it is, I hold fast to my beinghood and struggle against becoming diffused into oblivion. I, the Guardian of the Ocean, cannot feel myself to be a successful guardian if my ocean is dying; therefore, my spirit considers allowing itself to be blown to the Four Winds, never to be personified again.

The seas and oceans are affected also by the rapid melting of the ice caps. This further creates a state of confusion and chaos for me, and within the waters of Earth. Major ocean currents are changing rapidly after remaining the same for thousands, even millions, of years. Ocean creatures die because suddenly the water is too warm or too stormy. On top of the crisis created by humankind with the greenhouse gases (global warming), the sun is heating up further adding radiation and heat to a weakened atmosphere. We mention these specifics to arm you with full knowledge for a more successful Ocean Healing!

And, there is an entirely new development somewhere below the surface of my western Arctic Ocean; there is a layer of warm water which is expanding and rising. Your scientists are not sure how large it is or where its boundaries are, but one thing is certain: If it reaches my surface, under the ice cap, it could rapidly melt the ice cap!

The Arctic Ocean warming from **below** is an entirely new phenomenon. If this scenario reaches full fruition, it will spell a catastrophic Change Times. But this does not need to happen!

Human beings create the future for us all at this point. Tibus and his friends are giving you a blueprint for changing the future with the power of your mind and soul. Nothing is yet written in stone. In your meditations, work hard on healing my oceans and seas; create a positive outcome. Cool the waters, clean the waters! Heal the sea creatures, empower their life force.

Your mind has more power than you can possibly imagine!

This is the Guardian of the Oceans; I wish you, "God speed."

Note from Diane:
Do you realize that humankind has triggered the extinction of:
> *one-fourth of all the birds on the planet,*
> *one-sixth of all the mammals,*
> *one-twelfth of all the plants,*
> *one-twentieth of all the fish.*
Let's wake up and get it right in the Healing Millennium!

CHAPTER THIRTY-ONE:
WARS AND RUMORS OF WARS

This is Tibus. I come to you in love and light.

Each of you is aware of the crisis, or proclivity toward crisis, of the United States and Iraq, and of the United States and China. The Change Times is an empty canvas, waiting to be painted; the only colors available for this canvas are shocking purples. electric blues, screaming greens, bright reds, and gaudy yellows.

Before The Change Times, the colors usually available for the reality canvas were drab, quiet ones. However, The Change Times, by definition, offers a reality canvas of only very potent colors. Extremes.

Because of the chaotic momentum by which events happen during this time, we can forecast that "old rivals" (opposites), are bound to have confrontations.

Throughout humankind's history, East and West have been opposites, and have been often at odds with each other. The two opposites have developed archetypical personas which entered the mass subconsciousness long ago. These archetypes have spiritual and psychic power. For instance, to Westerners, "The East" is often mysterious and frightening. It is an entity which can induce the fear of the unknown, or obsessive love.

In daily reality, the people of The East live, work, and die with the same basic feelings as people of The West. But, the human race seems always ready to perceive what is different and frightening rather than what it has in common with other members of the species. The race does not celebrate or cherish its small differences. This "instinct" will be upgraded as humanity evolves spiritually; the rays which govern this facet of Man's consciousness, will be raised.

During The Change Times, every opposite which exists in the mass human consciousness must have a confrontation with its "other." This confrontation need not result in nuclear war or hand to hand combat. You must tackle this confrontation; think, feel, and work it out together, unite as a species, and finally and forever overcome your fear of "the other."

Male and Female is another example of "opposites" which are on the battleground of The Change Times. The fact that The Creator Spirit is made up of male and female components (energies), must be addressed by the human race, and then embraced. For millennia, the majority of the humankind has worshipped only half a God (the male half). No wonder humanity is not doing well! A notable exception is the Eastern Yin/Yang belief.

Another Male/Female issue: In the late Twentieth Century, humans are trying to come to grips with gender identity and sexual preference. Spiritual evolution will mean that you will no longer stand in judgment over another individual's preference or feelings on this very personal subject.

There is no inherent evil in gender identity or sexual preference, this concept needs to be thrown out with witch burnings and heretic drownings.

114

In 1996, the East/West confrontation heated up with rumors of an imminent nuclear attack on Los Angeles, launched from China. The flash point would have been the issue of Taiwan; does it return to Chinese control or does it remain independent?

However, this crisis quickly disappeared from the fabric of reality. Did the prayers, meditations, and positive energies of worried but enlightened people all over the world, help diffuse this crisis? I can tell you unequivocally, the answer is, "Yes!" You must realize that enlightened people joining together spiritually has already made a huge, positive difference in this particular timeline."

"In this particular timeline" is another way of saying, "in this particular alternate reality".

Another confrontation which must occur in the extremity of The Change Times, is the Christian/Moslem conflict. The Change Times "demands" that this be the case; chaos, and the death throes of the old, dark energies, hover around this situation. It is as if all of humankind's worst feelings and actions, are drawn magnetically to this archetypical confrontation.

A closely related "cauldron of unsolved conflict" is the Jewish/Moslem animosity. Other examples of on-going conflicts of opposite energies during these Change Times are the Ireland/England and the Hindu/Moslem conflicts. It is almost as if these ancient opposite energies have to fight it out to the end of the unraveling dimension, because after that, the cloud will have lifted and there will be no more motivation or reason, to fight.

But until the human spiritual frequency is raised and a new dimension is entered, all the demons, ghosts, and apparitions of the old mass consciousness will keep popping up as never before.

Hatred is a demon which needs to be exorcised from the mass consciousness. Putting stereotypical tags on others is the ghost of the unenlightened human heritage of these recent dark millennia.

Perceiving another's religion to be wrong, whereas your is, of course, right, is a dying apparition of the old low frequency.

We wish to stress that there are many good aspects of humankind even now; there are the traits of bravery, tenacity, individuality, and curiosity. These will go with humankind into the risen frequency, becoming stronger than ever before.

It is never the objective to sterilize the human race or to make it a drab but peaceful imitation of its original self. Consider each of the Seven Rays of Human Consciousness; these will not change or be eliminated. However, you (not us), will simply raise their intensity, their radiance, their frequency.

We discover as we consider this confronting "the other" syndrome inherent in The Change Times, that every dark cloud indeed has a silver lining. The United States and Iraq, for instance, must confront each other at this moment in history, in order to advance and evolve. These confrontations are bound to happen and when they do, the door is opened to raise the frequency. Otherwise, the door remains closed. It is up to you to make that change a positive one.

Remember, change is a commodity you can never perceive as it happens;

you can never "catch" change in the act. It is either just before, or just after, change.

Now is the time to change the old archetype of the East/West opposites in the human consciousness. Embrace and celebrate that these differences exist; be no longer afraid of these differences. You will be achieving **change**, but remember, it is very elusive to perceive until it is over. Create rays of enlightenment across Mother Earth and soon this change will be reality. Change can occur in a sweeping, extreme way, only when the door is wide open; it cannot occur when things are drab, quiet, and stagnant. These are the days of intense, electrical colors on the canvas of reality. Be brave; do not become frightened as the parade of "the crisis of opposites" marches on.

May the healing light of goodness surround you, always,
Tibus

NOTE FROM TIBUS ON GERM WARFARE AND BIOLOGICAL WEAPONS

As you know, my friends, germ warfare did tragically affect many soldiers of Desert Storm, despite the fact that this truth was kept secret, then denied, for several years by the government. They still have not faced up to the entire situation. Our prayers go out to all those affected by this terrible germ warfare.

Iraq does of course have an abundance of biological weapons which can affect a huge area. They could kill all human life (including their own), and many other kinds of life, with their stockpile of biological weapons.

It may seem to Saddam Hussein that he would "only" be giving the people of the U.S. anthrax, but I can promise him, he would die of the same dreaded outbreak within a few weeks. If pushed into a tight corner, Saddam will not act rationally, even for his or his people's survival, and so the terrible vision which Nostradamus saw, would become reality.

But, remember, my friends, prophesies and predictions are given so that the future can be changed. It is not written in stone, this nightmare need not happen!

Prophesies in themselves have no reason to exist unless they are given to us as a warning of what path not to take. They do give a possible future reality, but they do not give the only reality. Nostradamus himself would concur with this; it is the only way his life and his work were not in vain.

Your prayers, meditations, and stream of thought can upgrade the mass consciousness. You see, your prayers, meditations, and stream of thought **are** the mass consciousness! Even though someone such as Saddam is almost impossible to reach (to upgrade) as an individual, you can create a reality around him which is not conducive to his mania. Create a reality around him in which his power wanes and his people turn away from him. Many do not truly support him as it is. Make him a tempest in a teapot, a teapot to which no one gives any importance. His mentality is that of the old dark days, and they are fast spinning into oblivion.

The human species will go into The Healing Millennium without its little tyrants and its pathetic dictators.

At this time, we also issue a warning regarding the situation with North Korea, especially where the use of nuclear weapons is concerned. Include this crisis area in your meditations. It is interesting to note how many people feel alienated from the United States political scene. There seems to be no right choice to make. This is further proof that the daily dimension is unraveling.

The People are wiser than their politicians assume them to be. There are a huge number of silent but very aware individuals in the U.S. as the century draws to a close. You will make yourselves known and heard when you see the window of change, opening. It is encouraging to know how many people see through the false agendas fed to them by their governments.

Governments should only be there to serve the needs of the people; once they become self-perpetuating and self-serving, it is time to discontinue them.

The main barrier to discontinuing a government is that The People cannot seem to unite for even a limited period, and work together. Each perceives that his welfare is a separate issue with different needs from his neighbor. Thus, citizens fight with each other or feel fear for each other, rather than together, discontinuing the government which is the real culprit.

This inability to unite will ease as the frequency is raised and the small differences between people begin being perceived as positives rather than negatives.

One of the conflicts inherent in The Change Times energy, is "The People" as opposed to "authoritarian government." This is why it seems bureaucracies are falling apart, becoming more absurd and unable to function. They belong to the old frequency and are perhaps its most absurd creation. Therefore, bureaucracies are among the first vestiges of the old, dark, frequency, to fall apart.

You might be thinking, "Why worry because this whole thing is coming to an end anyway!" But I emphasize that it will not come to a satisfactory end in your particular timeline, if you do not make it so. You are making the future, my friend!

And while this statement is always true of everyone, I assure you that enlightened people such as yourself have much more to do with weaving reality than is "normal," and this is especially true in these chaotic times of change.

You are powerful psychically because of your enlightenment; you are a powerful weaver of the fabric of Space/Time.

May the healing light of goodness surround you, always,
Tibus

CHAPTER THIRTY-TWO:
REALITY, THE INTERNET, AND A WARNING

This is Tibus. I come to you in love and light.

Reality is composed of The Physical and The Spiritual. The bridge between these two is The Mind. The Mind creates The Physical, but The Spiritual is infinite and not subject to The Mind's whims of creation. We must therefore always remember, that although the physical ramifications of vast global climate change and other man-made and natural threats seem to be progressing at a frightening and intensified pace, our **spiritual** influence on reality is capable of off-setting the physical half of reality.

We still can change future reality to the positive. It is not too late. Above all, the human race must reach out to other humans and other life forms. Humankind must care on a soulful, instinctive level.

Otherwise, no matter how great the intellect is, it will lead to oblivion. An example of this is the advanced technology humankind has developed; it leads no where but to "the end."

I have never claimed that every human on the face of the Earth is capable of spiritual evolution at this time. Sadly, we all know this is not the case.

But, it is the human race as a whole race who will take the step upward, whether there are billions of humans left, or only a handful.

It is not about one individual who manages to develops the most psychic powers. I can promise you that for every human with "highly developed psychic powers," there are a thousand aliens out there with a hundred times the psychic power. And for every human who considers him or herself of "high intellect," there are a thousand aliens who are a hundred times as smart. It is about who can love unconditionally; who can care on a deep spiritual basis. No being in the universe can aspire to love "more" than unconditionally! No race has more potential to care on a deep spiritual basis, than humankind!

It is not about becoming a being who can zap others with the wave of his finger. It is about becoming an individual who will reach out to help his dying Mother World and all her life forms.

It is about becoming a being who will not, in the future, make the same stupid mistakes as his ancestors made.

It is: Doing to others as you would have them do unto you.

You may become a super being in terms of IQ and even psychic power, but if you do not understand this truth, and take it to heart, you may well end up in Hell itself, a world composed of only you, a mind all alone. This is the worst of all scenarios.

I wish to state my concern regarding The Internet: Not only is this "entity" driving book publishers and bookstores out of business at an alarming rate, and opening assorted other Pandora's boxes, it is a way for "Big Brother" to know your personal data and interests. It is not as private as you feel it to be when you log on!

In the future, it will prove to be a real danger for a number of you who travel its "highways." Also, it tends to make you reach out less to others in real ways; it tends to make you a "one man universe."

In a number of ways, The Internet leads away from enlightenment. Please do not get too heavily into it without giving it deep thought; allow your own intuition and your spirit guides to give in-put on this subject. Do not rely on mere intellect or blind curiosity.

Cherish the human invention called, "a book," and enjoy reading wondrous books whenever you can.

The ability to read is a gift given to humankind and to no other life form on the planet. It is one of your most precious possessions, this ability to read. Knowledge is precious. From it, springs wisdom itself when blended with experience. Be sure you have a quality source from which to read; do not settle for shallow, commercial items when doing that magic act called "reading."

May the healing light of goodness surround you, always,

Tibus

CHAPTER THIRTY-THREE:
FACING FEAR AND PARANOIA

This is Tibus. I come to you in love and light.

We refer again to the analogy about Earth and The Change Times upheavals: "The dog is shaking her fleas." Should we not try at all to quell Earth's anger, letting her shake to the maximum, and if it gets rid of the human race in the process, good riddance? But, no! It is always preferable to work for the good, the peaceful outcome. If your dog is covered with fleas, do you let him shake and rub himself into insanity, doing damage to himself more than the fleas? No, you calm his shaking and offer enlightened help to him.

It is our fervent belief that the human race is worth saving and that your potential as cosmic citizens is unlimited. I myself speak to you as a product of The Future. It has also been said that some form of life on Earth will survive, even if there is a nuclear holocaust or similar cataclysmic disaster.

Yes, the cockroach will survive a nuclear disaster but are not the leopard, the tortoise, the panda and the whale, preferable creatures to the cockroach in most ways? Just because some primitive form of life would survive (short of the planet breaking into tiny bits), this is no reason not to care!

If the planet were to leap backward in terms of life forms, this is not what she wants and it is not in the course of natural evolutionary momentum.

Earth must go forward, not backward. You must not stand idly by while all (or nearly all) is destroyed when you have the power to make a brighter, better day. The Healing Millennium will happen, but will your branch of reality (your timeline) be a part of it?

The God Spark which burns within you gives you the right and the responsibility to "interfere" in what is happening. After all, the human race has interfered in the natural scheme of things, causing this crisis.

This is not a crisis brought on by the natural march of evolution; Earth naturally has many millions of years of golden health and youth before she becomes an old, tired world.

The mutated frogs which keep appearing in Midwestern states tell the story: This is not natural, not of The Creator's design!

You must cut through all the static of global conspiracies and UFO abduction scenarios, true though some may be, and work toward the reality of raising the frequency. This will make every government agency, every conspiracy, every negative alien in cahoots with the military, extinct!

I have had to remind Diane of this at various UFO and New Age conferences as she has run into more than her share of strange, fearsome stories told by frightened people. One can get paralyzed by fear, which is truly our greatest enemy.

Even taking all that is told by frightened or paranoid people at face value, I remind you that individuals cannot go up against a government or a strange shadow government, or negative aliens, on their terms. These entities have more fire-power, more computers, more evil. So what is the answer?

The Answer: You must turn the page! Leave them behind in the old mundane dimension. Make their greed and negativity as out of date as using leeches for blood-letting and as antiquated as burning enlightened people as witches.

People who get trapped in the Fear Syndrome and who scoff at those who are trying to raise the frequency, fail to realize that humankind has risen before out of The Dark Ages and into the Renaissance which celebrated freedom, the human form, and diversity. Humankind has proven he can turn toward the light many times before. Granted, this turning of the page will be an even bigger "turn," one which elevates "Homo sapiens" to "Homo cosmos," but leaps of consciousness have been made before. When did it happen that Neanderthal and Cromagnon became Homo sapiens? It did happen!

You do not have thousands of years for a slow evolutionary change because of the tragic state of the Mother Planet. Therefore, some of you must make a huge leap, from past to future, from darkness to light. Everyone who can make the leap, will.

We do not choose you, you choose yourself!

Of course as an enlightened soul, your choice is inevitable. It is easier than you might imagine, just as winter turns to spring, and night turns to day. Join us as brothers and sisters in the cosmic community.

May the healing light of goodness surround you, always,
Tibus

CHAPTER THIRTY-FOUR:
TELEPATHY AND EMPATHY

THOUGHTS FROM DIANE:
I often wonder at the fact that most people don't seem to care or pay much attention to the many obvious crisis, both natural and man-made, which are happening right before the millennium changes.

Things are really falling apart! Governments should be spending most of their resources in helping us prepare, and newspapers should have daily headline news on various potentially catastrophic situations.

Granted, maybe there is no need to cause panic, but Earth's citizens have a right to know and to truly comprehend what is going on, because there are spiritual, emotional, and physical efforts which can be made to help the situation and to survive. Of course, what is happening is so enormous that it spells the end to government, church, and other institutional control of The People; this reflects the true reason they do not let people know what is happening.

Also, maybe by definition this has to be a "people's movement," one which springs out of the heart and soul of each individual. Though there is chaos and change outside, The Change Times is really about inner changes. So perhaps I should be glad that "outer forces" such as governments and the media, are not championing the reality and meaning of The Change Times.

Of course, governments have their own agendas and this above all, is the frightening aspect to that part of the Change Times which is outside nature's realm. Secret government agendas and collusion frighten and anger me more than all Mother Nature has to throw at us.

I love, respect, and understand Mother Nature and her anger. The human-made world of greed, deceit, conspiracy, and cruelty is alien to me and to any enlightened individual.

This is Tibus. I come to you in love and light.

One thing we know: As Earth's time of change careens along, we need each other more and more! We realize that you turn your eyes skyward with even greater urgency, but the need is not all on your side of things. We of the higher realms need you also. You may not realize that you are our eyes, ears, and emotions, on Earth. We love you as equals and friends, and I do not aim to sound like we are "using" you, so let me explain:

Part of your Assignment: Earth is that you live within the human timeline, as human. And because we are in telepathic contact with each of you to varying degrees, we can then witness events and feelings with the greatest emotion and empathy.

As the Change Times unfold dramatically, your human eyes and ears record these events and react to them. The best way for us arrive at the greatest empathetic understanding is through being in telepathic contact with you. We see what you see, hear what you hear, we laugh when you laugh, and we cry when you cry.

Our contact with you allows us to empathize and to understand in ways we could not possibly do without you. This in turns allows us to better know how to help. We are not cold emotionless aliens, but no matter how sensitive and empathetic we are, we cannot feel as we would if it were happening to us, as human beings of the late Twentieth Century.

As an analogy to the point I am making:

Even though you felt sympathy for the people in China who have recently suffered major flooding, you probably became more emotionally wrapped up in the recent floods in U.S., such as the ones along the Red River in the Dakotas and Minnesota.

This is human nature; indeed, it is the nature of any life form to be more emotionally involved with its immediate tribe and environment. This is your Earth, not ours, and you are living it first hand. Being at a distance, no matter how great our technology, creates a certain objectivity and scientific attitude.

We do not want this. We are spiritual beings as well as advanced technical beings, and we truly wish to share Earth's travails. We do not want to merely sympathize, we must empathize. The more we share, the more we are able to help, because the power of our prayers, meditations, and our physical efforts (projects), have then more intense emotion, commitment, understanding and effort. The "remoteness" factor is removed.

For years I have urged you, my human friends, to get in touch with your own star guardians or spirit guides. Guardians are here/there for you, but you must first make the simple effort of tuning to the right spot on the frequency dial. If you do not make the effort to recognize our existence, we will not be real within your life. It is as if there was a radio station you should listen to, but you would not twist the dial to find it.

Allow me an analogy: In the 1940s, when the U.S. military showed a film to Pacific Islanders on how to make a sanitary latrine, the island people watched the film and enjoyed it. They saw chickens, they saw people, they saw trees. But they did not perceive, let alone comprehend, the making of the latrine, because this concept was not in their consciousness. In the same way, you must incorporate and become aware of, spirit guardians in your consciousness and perception.

Just to feel your spirit guide's presence at a precious moment, is enough. It is also wonderful to actually receive a communication from him or her, or to perceive a vision of the special friend in the higher realms.

There must be that telepathic link, that **knowing**, between you and your guardian. You may not have realized that this helps us better perform our work for The Light, as well as giving you guidance, protection, and love. Believe me, it does!

Telepathy does not have to hit you over the head in order to exist in your life. Most times, it is very gentle; you can hardly tell the difference between your own thoughts and the thoughts that we send to you.

Many people feel they receive nothing from us telepathically but this is because they simply cannot identify our telepathy from their own thoughts. They are expecting a booming voice in their head, but this is not the way we work.

People who have "booming voices" in the head often end up in institutions, and this is not our plan for you, my friend. Our contact with you must therefore be more subtle, gentle, and unobtrusive.

Only entities of negative intent do not care about their human contacts; many humans who seek or passively accept contact with negative entities do end up in institutions.

You may not have encountered us positive guides in person, but there is that soulful love which simply exists on its own, regardless of time, world, or condition, between guardian angel, and human friend.

Finally, I do want you to know that we are aware how much you need us in terms of emotional comfort and strength as the days become more and more frightening. Never doubt that we are here for you; it is really very simple to activate the link and to reach us. Sometimes we activate the link but you are snowed under with life's daily static. Do not be frustrated if you feel you have not yet accomplished a telepathic link with your special one on high.

We are as natural and available as the air you breathe. The need to be in contact is mutual; we need you, too. At no time are we haughty, aloof, or pompous. Contacts who seem to have these characteristics are usually negative entities masquerading as positive beings. They cannot keep their ridiculous egos out of the equation. Have you suspected that we star guardians are "around," or that our spiritual presence is with you? You are correct; in fact, we are with you much more than you realize. Simply turn your dial to our frequency; do so consciously.

Our love is unconditional. Turn to us, because we are here/there for you!

May the healing light of goodness surround you, always,

Tibus

CHAPTER THIRTY-FIVE:
DIANE'S TIPS ON SURVIVING THE FINAL DAYS

THE MIND AS A REDUCING VALVE:

Sometimes I feel that the "daily world" is the most extreme reality which my conscious mind can manufacture in order to sabotage my spiritual ascension.

It is said that the conscious mind functions as a "reducing valve," screening out almost everything in the entire universe, and leaving what it can handle, which isn't much. It dwells on all the petty, detailed stuff which composes the daily world.

If it is true that we not only perceive our reality but participate in it, then my conscious mind apparently enjoys manufacturing daily problems, hassles, and crisis, which keep me from taking that next step up the awareness ladder; my conscious mind is afraid and insists on being "safely" planted on the ground. However, I am not totally discouraged with my conscious mind and its infamous reducing valve, because I have managed, thus far in life, to survive this insane daily reality, and (sometimes), I handle it fairly well.

An example is my move back from Ireland with my fifteen cats, and two big dogs, in 1995. That was a truly absurd daily challenge which I created for myself. Did I really need that kind of a challenge? The encouraging aspect is, I survived it! Looking back, I am even proud of having done it. All fifteen cats and two dogs made it safely from County Cork, Ireland, to Joshua Tree, California, via car, plane and then U-Haul across country. Isn't there a saying, "God loves a fool?" I would certainly qualify.

As you can see, I have decided that I can create some doozies when it comes to mundane challenges; the above is only a small example of the challenges of my life thus far. I figure I have the right to consider myself an "expert" on surviving and handling daily disasters and challenges by this point in my life; I now offer my "expertise" as we reach toward raising The Seven Rays of Human Consciousness.

I hope what I have to say will help you as we live through the final gasp of the old, dark dimension. Know that you are not alone in struggling through absurd situations these strange days. I certainly don't have all the answers and sometimes I wonder if I'll survive this insane world, let alone give guidance to others. "What can go wrong, will go wrong," is Murphy's Law in this dimension.

Humor is the key to surviving it, and thus my contribution to this effort will reflect this truth. I refuse to dignify the daily absurdities of the old millennium by approaching them without a certain humor.

As I work with fellow star people, I have found that those who retain their humor, also retain their sanity and their psychic/spiritual strength. Without humor, the world becomes a paranoid place and the person can only center on "me." The greater, universal "I AM" is lost. The daily world is the "overlay sheet" which humankind has foolishly placed over the real universe. It blocks the real light from shining through and it is full of petty rules, laws, hassles, distractions, bureaucracies, and computer errors. The last days of the old millennium is the freeway with its ten car pile-up; it is the voice on the phone which tells you that you owe $5000.00 on a certain credit card when you don't even have that card.

It is the threat of having your home robbed and your life threatened in a terrifying "home invasion" and it is that flat tire on your car when your spare is also flat. It is that most annoying commercial on television and it is the sadness of watching the big tree which has stood in town for hundreds of years, being cut down.

The closing days of the old millennium are all this, and unfortunately, more.

As a writer, I feel I have an advantage, because writers tend to put events and people into stories, even if it is only in our heads. And once you consciously put daily hassles into "stories" in your head, half the battle is won. This gives you balance and perspective. This gives you an overview. This gives you humor. These are the survival tools you need as the dimension around you continues to unravel.

The worst thing that can happen to you in these chaotic days, is that you get lost in the trees and cease to perceive the entire forest. This means also that you have lost your humor. Everything becomes deadly serious; life becomes an endless uphill struggle in which you never reach the top of the hill. Injustices will abound.

If daily life in these last days of the old millennium is getting to you, try writing a story about it in your head, or put it on paper; actually list all that has gone wrong and all that is, as yet, unfinished. Also list the positive aspects of your life.

Allow yourself an ironic smile. Or even, a good laugh. Laughter is wonderfully healing.

In this way, you will be separating yourself from the daily problems by just an inch or two. You can extricate yourself from the middle of them, becoming untangled to some degree. Thank goodness for perspective!

We all agree that "money" is enough to make us come unhinged. It is seldom a laughing matter. But the conscious act of removing yourself from its grasp (or the worry about lack of it), is in itself very healing and empowering. Make a statement to "money" so that the universe can hear, "Money, you do not own me, you will not kill me, and I will not jump through your hoops! I have the power, not you!"

Regain your inner balance and centering. Feel the Whole You who is the cosmic being. Touch the God Spark within. Know that you are more than this fatigued, stressed individual who worries about money or other daily problems. Yes, you are much more than this!

With balance and perspective comes humor, new energy to tackle old problems, and a slight "remoteness" from the silly daily routine. You will no longer be so vulnerable to being hurt.

The "overlay" which is the old dark dimension which humankind has created for itself, will lift, and we will soon see The Creator's future millennium shining through. The vibration of The Seven Rays of Consciousness gains momentum; we renew that magical commodity called Hope. We are rejuvenated.

Star Woman

Artist: Pat A. Davey

125

How to Re-establish Your Centering

The art of "centering" is a miraculous spiritual tool which you must master as the final days of the dying millennium ebb away. It is an essential survival mechanism for the inner you. To master the art of "centering" also helps you toward raising the seven aspects (Seven Rays) of your consciousness so that you and The Healing Millennium, can co-exist together. Those who do not raise the seven aspects of their consciousness, will not exist in this new dimension; they will not be able to adjust to its vibration or magnetism.

Centering is such a simple mechanism; it is not difficult to do. Animal friends naturally center themselves after an upsetting experience; one of my cats sucks on my sweatshirt after an upsetting experience such as being taken to the vet's. Often your canine friend has a favorite corner in which to sit and "get himself together." Tibus assures me that beings of higher realms also need to center themselves from time to time. The art of spiritual centering is a commodity which they treasure; it opens a direct conduit to the Creator Spirit. It allows them to feel the God Spark within.

Take time to figure yourself out, take time to consciously realize what brings you simple spiritual happiness. Centering is simply the art of "getting yourself together" at soul level.

Sometimes an enlightened individual goes through a lifetime helping others but never makes the simple analysis of what brings him or herself, a feeling of serenity. If this is true, the individual may become "lost" eventually, wondering what his lifetime effort has been all about.

Enlightened people are by nature, "givers." But you must give yourself a gift as well. You must take time to center yourself and you must find the best way to do it. This is especially urgent in these final days before the dawn.

Centering is very important as a first step when meditating. However, you do not have to meditate every time you center yourself. Just the beautiful feeling of regaining your spiritual centering is goal enough; this helps your physical health as well, lowering blood pressure and alleviating stress. Stress is one of the main underlying causes of cancer, heart disease, and several other major enemies of your physical body. You should take time to center yourself often.

Centering is a feeling of being at home within one's soul. There is a moment of peace, and you are simply at ease. Suddenly, you can feel love again. Centering often causes you to sigh deeply and contently, letting go of the wears and tears of the day. You might also think of centering as "a stop to smell the roses." When you hold a six week old kitten in your hand and she starts to purr, and you then feel like purring, too, that is centering! It is that feeling of embracing your child with feeling rather than giving him a small hug because you "should."

Centering is the "spiritual glue" of your being; there will be much which tries to pull your being apart. The world will constantly wage war on your natural spiritual equilibrium. The ability to reach within and literally feel the soul, is all important in the chaotic days ahead.

Our animal friends and Mother Nature retain their natural state of balance (centering), and so you can look to them, as I do, for instant and miraculous centering.

When you were a young child on a warm summer day, the flowers smelled sweet and the sky was so blue, and you were centered. You felt Oneness with The Creator Spirit without even realizing it; in fact, you were the Creator Spirit!

Since that day in paradise, things have gone downhill quite often, haven't they? Financial worries. Relationship troubles. Sexual success, or lack thereof. Legal hassles. The list is endless.

What we need these days is that "quick fix" which gives us our centering, our balance, our perspective. Of course, we should also take time for the deeper, longer experiences, but in practicality, this cannot happen everyday.

For me, one of the quickest and best re-centering mechanisms is to bring The Pooka Cat into my office, which is the one room in the house in which the animals are not allowed. The Pooka and I stretch out on the sofa and commune. I love all my animal friends but this particular cat has a certain magic for me. In a sense, he is my soul, walking around in a black and silver marmalade fur coat.

The Pooka seems to know all this. Perhaps I am also his soul walking around as a human? The Pooka works his magic on me without fail. I stroke him, talk to him, feel the essence of his being.

Another of my favorite centering methods is to take a walk in my ten acres of North Iowa land. If the weather is alright, this can be the best method when I really need to get out of the house. Sunrise and sunset are pure magic. I look over the distant meadows and fields, and then I focus on my land. I comfort myself with thinking that this land will not be destroyed by a bulldozer. I watch the pheasants, the deer, the song birds, the barn cats. A sense of quiet comes over me. Time does not exist. Peace.

I am not a handy person at craft or sewing skills. But some people find their centering through knitting or making a particular piece of art or handicraft. This is not directly "nature" but it is natural in the broader sense; it allows the natural human body, mind, and spirit, to create.

For me, my two favorite methods of centering allow me to actively feel love, whereas moments before, I had probably grown numb toward feeling much of anything. Daily life does that to a person. You cope. You deal with occasional crisis. You struggle with constant petty details and boring tasks which are almost worse than a crisis. Activities like watching television or driving in little traffic, can calm you down sometimes. But watching television does not establish centering; it puts you into a mindless state which can be relaxing; but, there is no recognition of the soul. A calm drive in the car can come close to helping you re-establish centering, but a hike in nature is usually better.

Gardening or working with nature in some way, helps many individuals touch their soul as well. Also, some people find a state of serenity as they exercise.

If you have not been aware of your spirit's need to find centering each day, sometimes several times a day, start now to explore the miraculous art of centering. It is so easy, and works such wonders. However, you need to begin doing it, formally. Centering is one of the crucial keys to raising your spiritual frequency for The Healing Millennium. Each of The Seven Rays of Consciousness respond in a positive, upgraded way, during your special moments of centering.

If you do not find balance, perspective, and centering, you will have trouble coping with life, especially as the old dimension falls apart. Individuals who have mental breakdowns have forgotten their spiritual survival tools for finding serenity. They have lost the feeling of that God Spark within. Without this center, individuals unravel also. To center yourself is sometimes easier said than done, because the daily world puts many pressures on you to keep you from your God Spark. It is really a vicious circle: You try to establish centering, and the daily world tries to take it away. But the only way to survive the mundane world is to have your centering!

IS THE WORLD REALLY OUT TO GET ME?

Now that I have discussed the basic solution of, "Center yourself!" first, I am going to back track, and go over some of the bothersome aspects of life in the old daily dimension.

The first question might be, "Is the world really out to get me?"

Bad news! Yes, it may be. I remember that original **Star Trek** episode in which a giant organism in deep space perceived The Enterprise, and the crew aboard her, as invading viruses, sending antibodies to eliminate the invaders. The unraveling old dark dimension views enlightened individuals as "invaders."

Make no mistake, a dimension does have a collective consciousness. The daily dimension marches to the hum of "the mass human consciousness." This mass consciousness senses anything and anyone who is out of step, humming a different enlightened tune. Most of us have walked through life with a sense of alienation except when we commune with Nature or The Cosmos. Like that giant organism on **Star Trek**, the old, dark dimension tends to view us as threatening. We are invaders; we are aliens. We bring the frequency of peace, love, serenity, enlightenment, true freedom, and spiritual/psychic power.

How can government bureaucracies and other institutions remain as important as they demand to be, if our enlightened vibrations begin to dominate the frequency? Petty laws and rules will become insignificant on an enlightened planet; consequently, the whole system "dislikes" people like us. We do not fit in a comfortable niche or computer chip, and we threaten the status quo simply by existing.

The old dark dimension knows that its time is not long, and it resents the messengers of the Healing Millennium who already live in its world.

True, "the system" is not alive but it does have a collective cognizance about it. Enlightened folk simply do not regard it as the greatest or wisest voice in The Cosmos, so, it tends to be out to get us. We, unfortunately, stand out. This is true even though enlightened folk are not violent or breakers of significant laws.

The "props" of the daily world tend not to be our forte, either. We are often absent-minded, not oriented to thinking about all the daily details. Instead, we tend to be off watching a sunset or planting a seed. Or perhaps we are attending a UFO conference or taking a long walk. The Great Unknown fascinates us, whereas it is more socially acceptable to feel fear and hesitance about "strangeness."

Your spirit is wandering the stars. Your mind is one with nature. And with this spiritual dimension, you do just fine!

Perhaps I am going overboard to paint a picture of our enlightened alien frequency making us invaders in the dark millennium, but I have found that this perspective gives my humor a boost. Humor allows me to smile at my difference in this world, and in a smile, there is great strength and renewal.

This perspective also gives me a logical reason as to why daily life in the man-made world tends to be frustrating, trying to throw many curves my way. If I am expecting that curve ball, maybe I can avoid it.

Some people openly acknowledge themselves as aliens down here, thus they can laugh at how things are done on Earth. Others do not feel that they are aliens; they feel that they are human beings who can perceive an enlightened way, and who function in that way. Such individuals sometimes feel themselves to be aliens in time who would feel more at home in the ancient past, or in the future.

Which way is best for you? It is an individual matter. Whatever your soul tells you, is the viewpoint you should take.

I have known "Star Trekkers" who feel at home by role playing as Kirk and Spock on Earth assignment; a feeling of being at home on a starship often resonates with these people. Other individuals consciously long for their home planet, far away. Others proclaim themselves as "simply human" with a sprinkling of enlightenment. No way is the superior way of perceiving, and both "breeds" need reassurance and help in surviving daily life which is of a frequency not our own.

To consciously perceive why you feel different, and to take pride in your difference, is half the battle won.

I am one of the lucky ones who has taken my alienation and made a career of it, influencing others, hopefully to the positive. Perhaps I have made a small dent in the Great Wall of Ignorance. It has made its small dents in me as well.

I am positive that we can all turn our difference to a positive, helping create the higher dimension which we as a planet so badly need. Remember, The Healing Millennium will come, but we must reach out to jump on board, or it will not come for us. It is really an amazing catch-22.

We can take the conscious step of perceiving ourselves as voyagers sailing through the daily dimension, causing waves. These waves are waves to be proud of, and waves on which we can sail into the new dawn.

IS MOTHER NATURE MY FRIEND THESE DAYS?

I have a friend who feels that Mother Nature has promised her, that she (Nature) will never harm her. I feel the same way. This is not to say that I would feel completely at ease if I saw a hundred foot tidal wave headed toward me.

It is the same when we say we are protected by our star guardians and spiritual family: If I step in front of a freight train, I am not sure they would or could save me. But essentially, enlightened folk are protected by the higher realms who know that we hold to key to the future.

Nature is our friend if we perceive her as "friend." She recognizes us as different from the greedy individuals, governments, and corporations which harm her and which tend to inherently fear her.

These days with the global climate in a state of drastic change, we may feel threatened sometimes by Mother Nature. Torrential rains, floods, blizzards, tornadoes, record heat, the list is endless. We can feel the planet's anger and desperation. We wonder when earthquakes and volcanoes will strike and if we are in a safe place.

At this time in particular, it is very important not to become alienated from Mother Nature. Do not begin categorizing her with the old daily dimension; that is, don't feel they are both causing you lots of hardships and problems.

This may well be true, but it is imperative that you keep your channels open to Mother Earth and her living spirit, Gaia. Communicate with her, love her, send healing to her. It is important both for her, and for you.

If you are like me, Mother Earth is my "All" in terms of spiritual fulfillment. I must keep channels open to her just as I must eat and drink to stay alive. Take active, conscious steps to mend whatever wall might have developed between you and Mother Earth. If you have begun to fear her power, calm your fear and embrace her with love, empathy, and healing.

The symbiosis between Mother Earth and enlightened human (her child), is one of the great beauties of the universe. Each is pivotal to the other's survival these days. Each reflects The Other in the mirror of reality.

THOUGHTS ON THE EMOTION OF ANGER

I understand Mother Earth's anger these days; I empathize with her. I feel it is important that we communicate to her that we do understand. Anger and frustration are perfectly natural. I have heard New Age people advise others to cleanse themselves of all anger, past, present, or future. I disagree that anger is automatically a negative emotion. Anger is a natural emotion, which usually occurs when there is an injustice or when you are very tired and frustrated.

The Spirit of the Volcano, B'Tamei, has explained that Mother Earth needs a vent for her anger and hurt. Our planet is not an emotionless being; we Earthlings, like our Mother, are not emotionless creatures, either.

I feel that even as we evolve, we will keep our range of emotions. We are Earth's children; her emotions will always be our emotions. To not show anger when an injustice is done, is to allow that injustice to be perpetrated without a whimper. When the world is perfect, only then will Earth's anger, and our anger, be unnecessary. It is true that we create our reality, but to try to stifle justified anger is not the answer; the picture is much more complex and vast than this.

Justified anger is a natural reaction; attempt to guide and control anger, do not let it rule you. You rule it. You should give this wise message to Mother Earth as well.

CAN I LOVE THE HUMAN RACE?

I have often tried to figure out if I love the human race, or hate it. Of course Tibus and my spiritual family guide me to love the human race, but I have to live down here! When I see someone mistreating a child or an animal, running over the living desert on a destructive dirt bike, driving too fast and recklessly on the freeway, or a million other "human" acts, I feel I might hate this impossible race.

I know that the human race has a "flip" side which is wondrously good. Humans risk their own lives to save children and animals. Humans work for years in a hostile environment to save the rhinoceros, and they donate their kidney to save another human's life. The list is endless.

In the 1960s, the Woodstock Generation loved everybody except their Draft Board. But that spirit soon wore thin when drugs were mis-used and lofty idealistic goals became warped and lost.

Just before Jerry Garcia died, my daughter and I went to a Grateful Dead concert and I was told many times by a very blissful young woman, "Everything is just as it should be, man. Everything is beautiful."

I wanted to say, "No, everything is not beautiful! They are turning this lovely national park over to a private firm to run for profit, the ice shelf is cracking, climate is going to hell, the government is rotten, and you are not in this reality anyway!" Then I realized that she still held the dream that I, too, held dear in the late 1960s.

To raise the frequency, should we simply believe we are in a perfect world, even if the daily world is going to hell? If perception creates reality, the theoretical answer is, "Yes." For me, it is a bit more complex. But at least I do believe that I must perceive the half full glass, where humanity is concerned, instead of the half empty glass. I choose to love this enigmatic species.

Keep a protective wall around yourself so as you are not taken advantage of or used. After taking a few basic protective measures, we must not be afraid to take the risk of loving. Ships are safe in the harbor, but that is not what they are made for. Yes, I choose to love the human race.

CHAPTER THIRTY-SIX:
PAST LIVES, SABOTAGE, AND REPEATING
SCENARIOS AS THE SEVEN RAYS INTENSIFY

Metaphysicians tend to explain reoccurring scenarios within an individual life as "karmic." This is true, although there seem to be as many versions of "karma" as there branches of religion.

If a person finds herself always the responsible one, while her sister is the irresponsible one, does this mean that the responsible sister was irresponsible in a past live? Or does it mean she has acted with responsibility, lifetime after lifetime; therefore, she also acts with responsibility now? I have heard it told both ways by people who were sure that they knew the answer.

I give past life impressions myself, so I am not criticizing the concepts inherent in past life impressions or the people who "read" them.

What I am saying, is that each individual ultimately must decide which past life or lives, make sense to his or her heart and soul. It is your choice as to which past lives scenarios you embrace, and this is a large part of what this exploration is all about. If you do have a scenario or situation which keeps occurring in your current lifetime, then it probably also occurred in past lives and is a lesson as yet unlearned.

Past life research can be particularly helpful in uncovering and understanding reoccurring scenarios in your present life. This exploration and knowledge is very important in knowing yourself on a soulful level; it is the kind of knowledge you need to raise the frequency of the Seven Rays and to move into The Healing Millennium.

Example: In your life on Earth, you realize that you always fall into the same pitfall in every job. You work harder than most other employees. You do not get much recognition, and it seems you get more than your share of criticism. Each job turns out to be the same.

Is this connected to past lives, wherein you did not learn to make yourself appreciated, either? Is this a lesson you have yet to learn? Or were you too egotistical in a previous life and have a lesson to learn in humility?

It is up to you to decide with heart and soul, which feels right; but, neither of these past life scenarios are of any use, unless they can help you consciously in your present lifetime. Each of us falls into familiar scenarios over and over again. Relationships are the most obvious of these, and we will tackle them in a moment. If you are to survive these final dark days and evolve into a new, higher frequency, then you must consciously identify the repeating scenarios which keep happening to you. You must know your soul this well!

If you are shy and get overlooked in this world, it matters not "how" you became shy but that you recognize your shyness as an essentially peaceful, gentle, positive trait which is not appreciated in this noisy world. From there, consciously work to assert yourself more while embracing your basic gentle nature, so that you are not caught in a constant "replay."

It is very important that do not try to change yourself drastically, being untrue to your soul, or begin to hate this trait in yourself. This gentle and positive trait is a part of you! Adjust the "shyness quotient" as you consciously come to understand its origins and reasons; embrace your soulful traits, because they lead to The Whole You.

Look at your present life from the over view. You see "the trees" every day and there are so many stresses and frustrations down among these trees! Rise up and look down on the forest from on high, to see your life's patterns.

There are patterns in your behavior and in the way others relate to you. Do you set yourself up to lose? Do you sabotage yourself? Many of us do!

Are you in the habit of living in a negative reality, thus subconsciously you begin to feel at home in a negative reality? If this is so, you sabotage reality every time it becomes positive. Does the negative reality feel comfortable and full of excuses? Have you ever ruined a nice new friendship when you managed to sabotage it without meaning to at all?

Sometimes we become accustomed to failure, comfortable in our daily abyss. We might study spiritual matters and really want to achieve enlightenment, but on a daily basis, we are our own worst enemy. We feel a negative reality is normal while a positive reality is living too close to the edge. The mundane grind can do this to one's perception after many years of struggling.

Even if we do not sabotage ourselves this badly, we all accept certain roles in certain scenarios which replay in life again and again. The Martyr. The Responsible One. The Hot Head. The Nice Guy Who Finishes Last.

Whatever the role, we learn to play it well, from early childhood onward. All the while, we limit our vista and our potential. If we rise above the forest, and look from on high at the role we learned, we can get control over the syndrome, and the repeating scenario it creates. The repeating scenario must not have control over us and our lives on Earth. Once we recognize the pattern, we have the power to overcome it.

CONSCIOUS RECOGNITION
OF WHAT PROGRAM WE SEEK REPEATEDLY IN RELATIONSHIPS

An example of the insight we are seeking to offer, is illustrated by the "co-dependent" concept. This way of relating to others usually begins in childhood and is carried into adult relationships. It may spring from past live experience as well, but our advice applies to the present, because this is where we need to survive.

A woman marries a man she knows to be abusive, she may have co-dependent characteristics. She is attracted to this type of man because she can comfortably play the only role she knows how to play in a relationship, despite the fact she is miserable. This is the role she has known all her life, usually beginning with her relationship to her father.

If a man marries several women who are alcoholics or substance abusers, it may be that he only feels comfortable in a relationship as the martyr, the suffering one, who holds things together. This is his comfort zone. He does not know how to need or how to be given to. He only knows how to give.

There are other, more illusive patterns which some of us seek. It might seem relatively simple not to get involved with someone who abuses substances, but in reality, it can take many years and much heartache to identify this pattern; and the more complex patterns are even harder to recognize.

With age comes wisdom but by this time, life has been lived.

Enlightened people have a particularly difficult time in pursuing their spiritual paths while maintaining happy relationships. Many times, there is someone at home who adamantly does not approve of spiritual curiosity.

There are any number of people in our **Star Network** who receive their newsletters at post office boxes because partners do not approve of their spiritual pursuits. Others would love to follow spirit quests, perhaps visiting a far distant land they are attracted to spiritually, but they must stay home to honor their role in a relationship or family.

There are any number of variations on this, but it is obvious that enlightened people (star people) are very subject to falling into restrictive relationships. Few, if any, of us seem to live easy lives as the one who is pampered.

Within the **Star Network**, there are those who work together as mates or as a family who are true soulmates and eternal partners. They pursue a dream together, such as trying to buy a special piece of land. But the daily dimension just loves to sabotage spiritual dreams, and inevitably, it is a real struggle in mundane terms, for these dreams to become reality. Banks, laws, lack of money, zoning rules, dishonest contractors, all seem to work together to keep dreams from happening. It takes great spiritual fortitude to pursue these dreams. However, how fortunate enlightened folk are who belong to a whole family of enlightened folk!

To identify the situation or scenario consciously, and to know you are not alone in your struggle, gives you a tremendous boost in psychic/spiritual power. You can then "over-ride the program" which the great cosmic computer seems to constantly run for you. You cannot beat the game if you don't know you what game you are playing.

An example of a "relationship program" which has run in my life, though I didn't consciously realize it until recently: I tend to fall for men who are seemingly worthy, noble people in very difficult, adverse situations; these are situations in which society has placed them. I want to be the helping hand, I want to be strong for them. Is that nice of me, or a bit condescending? Probably both.

Another repeating scenario which I follow: I fall for men from large, impoverished families, who are the second son of that family. Isn't that a silly pattern? But of the three men I have truly loved in my life, each fit this description. I did not consciously realize this until recently, when the third relationship was bitterly over.

True, there may be past life reasons, but the knowledge which helps me most today is that this is a syndrome, a "program" which I have had to deal with in the present lifetime. If the frequency of my Seven Rays of Consciousness is to intensify (rise), I must learn not to fall into the same "program" over and over again.

I am explaining this about myself in an effort to ask: Are there strange patterns in your "programming?" There is nothing wrong with this; in fact, it is wonderfully, intricately "human." However, we need to identify such patterns so we can gain control over them and not fall victim too many times to a broken heart. Or, even worse, so that we can be spared from a long term, destructive, negative relationship with a partner who ultimately is a mis-match and who destroys our loving nature. Daily life is difficult enough without misery at home; spiritual evolution cannot take place when we are personally unhappy.

We will probably always be attracted to someone who fills the need of our "programming" but we can learn to have control, not falling blindly every time. If we can do this, we are one step ahead in our struggle to survive and evolve.

CHAPTER THIRTY-SEVEN:
JUST BECAUSE I'M PARANOID
DOESN'T MEAN THEY AREN'T WATCHING ME

We who seek enlightenment are an interesting mix politically. I know some who are of the "new patriot" mentality and who believe in many of the global conspiracy theories. These friends have explained that they are not reactionaries or racists, but that we all know there is something terribly wrong. "We love our country, but not our government," they tell me.

I can understand this, especially considering some of the channeled information I have received. I find myself in agreement these days, with people who, at one time, "old liberal me" would have vehemently disagreed with.

I also passionately retain some liberal beliefs, especially where human rights and the environment are concerned. Of course, many New Agers are very liberal; some are so open and tolerant that they don't even believe in the antiquated political system anyway. These days, the old tags of "liberal" and "conservative," which worked as late as the 1970s, do not work at all. This is a whole new ball game with The New World Order threatening as an abhorrent monster to all of us.

Becoming paranoid about being singled out as "different" or "a radical" can make daily life a very miserable process. You feel constantly at war with your society, worried about who is bugging you and what Big Brother computerized list your name has gone onto, now.

A few years ago, I received an anonymous letter from Hawaii stating that, "You should know, your name has been upgraded on a list which was entered into a computer here." The writer didn't even know what subject of interest had earned me this dubious distinction; it might have been my interest in crashed saucers, it might have been my interest in Irish independence, or goodness knows what else, because I am always interested in strange subjects!

But, oh well, life went on with no real effects from this.

The "patriotic talk show" hosts refer laughingly to the lists they are on, the enemies they make. I admire their courage even if I do not agree with everything they say. In subscribing to New Age magazines, or adding your name to the health food store list, or in campaigning for a certain local candidate, or in a thousand other ways, you may have added your name to a list somewhere.

Don't worry about it! Their lists must have so many people by now that there is little efficiency. Who is left to do the "watching?"

Once in a while, someone does have a real battle with "them" which sounds like paranoia run amok but is all too real. One never knows when "they" are watching or when "they" finally go away. But if you are controlled by the possibility that "they" are watching for the rest of your life, there is no separating it from paranoia. You lose your humor and your ability to see events and yourself, in perspective.

Is this what "they" hope to achieve? There is nothing sadder than a very spiritual, enlightened person becoming self engrossed and awaiting the next psychic attack or "bug" in the lamp shade.

Of course, if there is an obvious reason, you should be careful and concerned, but, as daily life goes by, don't allow yourself to become a slave to paranoia or to conspiracy theories. Live in the Eternal Now. Find joy in the moment. Be aware and intelligent but don't worry excessively or obsessively, because you will only lose your humanity and spirituality along the way. Isn't this what "they" want?

In order to raise the frequency of the Seven Rays, you must not become bogged down in fear or paranoia, justified or not. Keep your sense of humor and your perspective. Center yourself often. Be unsinkable. Be indefatigable. Be inscrutable. Be invulnerable to "them."

Keep your joy and spontaneity. Keep your spirit. Keep your humanity.

Visualize a tree with massive roots. The roots are actually bigger than the above-ground part of the tree. When I need a bit of solace from the mundane world, I visualize myself as a tree. Her leaves get hit by bird droppings, dirt from the highway, chemicals from the factory, and insecticide from the fields nearby. Yes, the daily static, hassles, wear and tear, are formidable!

The analogy may become a bit silly, but, still, I find this a helpful visualization: My tree roots are deep in the fertile cosmic soil. So, despite the many knocks I receive, I remain a healthy, sturdy tree. I am very strong. I am a beautiful life form. Tibus and my other guides are my water. Nature is my nourishment. Even if my leaves become tattered from daily life, my roots remain untouched and strong. They are ready to renew me, to help me send out new, shiny leaves into the universe.

Enlightened folk are "sensitives" in a world which values and rewards insensitivity and greed. The Spiritualists consider an individual a "sensitive," when he or she is psychic and can "read" other people. We have "read" other people all our lives. We have acute vision. We are intuitive and psychic.

And therein lies our problem in enduring this crazy world. But therein also lies the factor which will save us. We must use our sensitivity to become conscious of all the games, programs, and patterns which happen as one experiences a lifetime. We then need to get control of them, escaping their control over us. This advances us toward the raising of our frequency. We must keep our sense of humor, our patience and serenity. But we do not have to be perfect in these areas. It is okay to breakdown, to feel tired, to feel angry. Let it go.

To regain centering is extremely important, both for daily sanity and for raising our consciousness toward the Healing Millennium.

That is where my analogy to the tree and her mighty root system comes in again. The tree is centered because of her roots. Your roots are spiritual. They are cosmic. They are natural. They are of a "star" orientation. Embrace these roots, be unconditionally proud of them, and let them be your reassurance and strength. Your roots and identity are precious and powerful.

In surviving this crazy, silly world, you are helping to create a new, better dimension. The Seven Rays of your consciousness will intensify and shine brightly, opening up that new dimension. This knowledge is enough to keep you fighting, and smiling. As an old friend who has since passed on to work in the higher realms, used to say, "Carry on!"

CHAPTER THIRTY-EIGHT:
A MESSAGE ON THE POLAR SHIFT

This is Mia-shee. I come to you as a snow sprite, and the source of my consciousness is firmly anchored in Earth's polar extremes. I am created by the force of electromagnetism. You might say, therefore, that I am an energy creature (energy animal). While I am a mystical creature (a winter nature spirit), I am also knowledgeable about the workings of physics and magnetic forces. Of course I would be, because these are the forces which compose "me."

Like you, there is a mystical me and a scientific me; my awareness is that the two do not contradict, but blend together to create The Whole. My cousin, the magnificent Aurora Borealis also knows these truths and she possesses a persona (a spirit) also. Watch her dance in the skies, along the horizon, whenever you are able.

I am more secretive than the Spring, Summer, and Autumn sprites, elves, gnomes, and such, but I am not this way in order to trick you.

The nature of Winter herself is one of dormant, hidden energy; During Winter, Nature enjoys serene rest and healing sleep; this is reflected in the peaceful beauty and quiet of a snow covered countryside. Underneath it all, Nature readies herself for the power and the miracle of Springtime.

When The Old Ways were the spiritual path of Earth, The Female was also reflected by the four "seasons" of The Moon: The Virgin (child), The Young Adult Princess, The Queen (middle-aged woman of mature beauty), and The Old Crone who was the elder woman of great knowledge and wisdom.

Winter is The Old Crone of Mother Nature's seasons, a time when it is alright to rest, when there is time to reflect and to feel one's hidden power, just beneath the surface. I, Mia-shee, reflect Mother Winter; my appearance is that of a tiny, old, white haired woman; still, I dance, sing, and celebrate in the snow because I am at heart, very young.

As Earth warms in these Change Times, Winter will still come to the northern places; blizzards will be common because of the increased moisture in the air which causes storm conditions in all seasons. However, we "entities of the cold" are ultimately threatened all across the globe because of this warming, stifling trend. We anxiously await The Dawn of the Healing Millennium.

Now, I would like to turn my attention to a more scientific area, one which speaks of electromagnetic energy. This I am very familiar with.

The Change Times, by definition, infers "opposites switching places" or a flip flop of reality (dimension). This involves the field of physics. In The Change Times, it will seem that the rules of physics will be inverse or reversed, in many instances.

When this begins to happen, remember all you have learned metaphysically and spiritually. Do not panic.

A "polar shift" has long been predicted for this time frame but few people realize the implications of a polar shift. It is not "just" a reversal of magnetic poles of the planet; it must be remembered that this in itself will affect the life force of the planet.

Each life spark is anchored in a "negative" or "positive" electromagnetic home base.

A polar shift will give an opposite polar base to every life-spark and life form. This does not mean that a good soul will become a bad one, because the terms "negative" and "positive" in this case, do not refer to spiritual goodness or badness.

Instead, they refer to the electromagnetic charge within each life-spark (the "physics" of the life-spark). To have life, the life-spark must have an electromagnetic charge of one polar magnetism or the other. This is a vital component of life.

This polar shift is one of the main reasons that the raising of the Seven Rays of Human Consciousness will occur in the near future. When electromagnetic charges flip-flop within a life form, it is extremely traumatic for that life form; however, any life form connected to Mother Earth/Father Cosmos will survive and eventually flourish. We say "flourish" because the shift injects new vigor and life.

This is another way of saying that The Healing Millennium is indeed coming! You have only to jump on board with the good intent of reaching higher awareness. The God Spark within will be the "commodity" which helps you survive and flourish. Be in touch with your God Spark within, and you will be alright.

This active link to The Creator must be there, however, or the life form will "drown" in the surging electromagnetic tide pools of this chaotic Change Time; the individual's beinghood will be swallowed into the waters of oblivion. By "oblivion" I refer to the fact that the consciousness will fade away, losing cohesiveness, into The Cosmos to be re-sculpted and re-created, eventually.

For those individuals in touch with their own God Spark (beinghood), with an active, vital link to The Creator Spirit, the time of polar shift leaves the door wide open to a dynamic, successful raising of frequency. The Healing Millennium awaits.

I AM Mia-shee. Be with me, the next time the snow flakes fall.

ADDENDUM: ELECTROMAGNETIC FORCES IN CEREMONIES

The Four Directions are excellent helpmates with which to work during meditation. North, South, East, and West are electromagnetic forces; we can also consider them as entities. Spiritually, The Four Directions are in harmony with the Four Phases of The Moon and The Four Aspects of The Female. The Four Elements (Fire, Water, Air, and Earth), are another mystical foursome.

All of these foursomes are powerful meditation, psychic helpmates. We will use The Four Directions as our example. When you visualize The Four Directions crisscrossing each other, the spiritual symbol of The Cross is formed. Using The Four Directions in meditation or healing ceremonies or rituals, is a very powerful action, because these are the electromagnetic elements of Gaia's being and of the Sky Father's universe.

Face The North and acknowledge and honor this entity. Do the same with each of The Four Directions. Work with each and then create a circle encompassing all of them. It is up to you to add specifics to this ceremony, because to have the greatest power, it must come from your own heart and soul.

Electromagnetism is easy to work with psychically; while it is a mysterious force, it has its specific, reachable energies. Psychic energy itself is interconnected with electromagnetic energy, and so the two are "naturals" together.

In **Earth Changes Bible**, we received a transmission from Elea, The Spirit of the Wind. As you work with The Four Directions in outside ceremonies, remember to include the Spirit of the Wind. You may be able to discern the ancient energies of the four aspects of The Wind: The North Wind, The South Wind, The East Wind, The West Wind. Place symbols on the ground, in the shape of a cross, to show each of these forces that you do indeed perceive and acknowledge them.

My enlightened friend, you take it from here!

CHAPTER THIRTY-NINE: THE CHILD WITHIN

(Thanks to a friend for sharing a reading in which this message appeared).
This is Tibus.. I come to you in love and light.
And so, move into the final two years of the 20th Century!

Over these past few years, your conscious awareness of who you are and why you are living in these times, in this place, has become clear and directed. This self awareness and self knowledge has become second nature, a real and vital part of your conscious identity, my enlightened friend.

You deal daily with concepts and knowledge which others would find hard to handle, and which you yourself would have been less able to handle just a few years ago. Now, the goal is clear and so is your spiritual identity. This in itself gives great psychic and spiritual power, and it gives great hope.

"Spiritual warrior" is a concept always worth contemplation and affirmation, now more than ever. This is what you are. We are happy to give guidance, counseling and healing, but we explain carefully that each individual has free will and the ultimate choice(s) must be your own.

The child must learn to tie his shoe, not let the parent do it for him every time. Because it is for you to choose this time, you are a spiritual warrior and pioneer. If it were all pre-ordained for you, there would be no need for being a warrior, no real exploration would take place.

As these Change Times proceed, you must learn not to believe every wild theory which you hear on a radio show or elsewhere. These are distractions, that is the least amount of harm they can do. At worst, they can be very damaging to your star path and that of the entire planet. It is up to you to choose what is valid.

Also, do not appoint a "leader" for yourself who then expects to dominate you and your beliefs. The Heaven's Gate cult is an example of individuals who gave too much power to a supposed leader. If you do this, you perform an act of self-sabotage; you stunt your cosmic journey in this lifetime. Trust your own inner guidance and intuition. Look in your own heart and soul for spiritual direction.

Of course you have teachers along the way; it is the best teacher who can gently nudge you along the path to being able to listen to your own heart and soul. Any teacher who pulls you further from this goal, is not the right teacher for you.

These are precarious times. To fall onto the wrong "New Age" path, such as

An alien friend awaits

Artist: Lynn Kristad

joining a cult which controls your life or, following the works of a personality who pushes his or her own ego, thus coming up with warped, inaccurate information, is just as bad as not bothering to "Wake up!" at all.

There have been pressures on both Diane and myself throughout these fifteen years, to become more extreme in what we say, more dominating, more egotistical. We are proud that we have steadfastly refused, and in fact, have become less egotistical than in the beginning. The pressures come mostly from well meaning individuals who want answers given to them on a silver platter, directly in front of their noses, so that they do not have to make choices for themselves. Or, so that they do not have to bother to explore much themselves.

Diane is a clear channel. We do not aim to be egotistical in stating this. A "clear channel" is one who can set him or herself aside during the channeling process. There are therefore no ulterior motives, such as getting control of the client in a cult-fashion.

Yes, I (Tibus) am subjective just as any other mind/soul is subjective, to its own perception. But at this fifteen year milestone, my guidance is tried and true in a number of ways, for a number of people. That is what I am here for, no more, no less.

Keep The Child close within conscious touch and memory. By "The Child," I mean the child in you, the you before puberty came and peer pressure started. It was then that life got more complex and soon the ups and downs of adult life became all-consuming.

This advice will serve you well: Think of the "young you" as The Child, know and love this individual well. Reach back to help this child; you more than anyone know what pain he or she suffered. You remember well the difficulties encountered in childhood. Sometimes the wise old-age you, the you who has lived this lifetime to its completion, reaches back to you today, comforting and advising you. Diane has gotten through the worst times of her life with the help of "the wise Old Diane."

This Old Diane shows up, not having been asked or even thought about; she holds and comforts Diane of the present. The Old Diane has embraced Diane at the moment of stress, hurt, or disappointment. The Old One has given her the nurturing and wisdom necessary to go on.

If you are not aware of this wonderful Old You, who offers help from another intersect point of Space/Time, help which is exclusively for you, please consider this concept. The Old You is always accessible, always cares, and is omniscient as to your entire life's path. In the same way, The Child is accessible as you reach back in Space/Time; you can be The Child's nurturing, comforting older friend, giving guidance when needed. Or, you can look to The Child for your own inspiration and renewed energy. The Child reminds you of what innocence is, of what really counts, and of how life is truly perceived before all the "slings and arrows" of adulthood.

Like a walk in Mother Nature, The Young You offers instant centering, balance, serenity. You might ask is there an Old Tibus and a Young Tibus, or am I ageless, or as old as anyone can get, or in some state of eternal youth?

The answer is, yes, there is an Old Tibus (The Old One) who advises and comforts me, and there is a Young Tibus (The Child) who is there to offer me innocence and clear perspective. Therefore, I am neither as old as anyone can get or in a state of eternal youth. Do not let there be an illusion of "being the victim" creep into your perception as the Dark Millennium draws to a close. By being completely accountable for your own life, you empower yourself. Know that others also must take their own inventory, and be accountable. Each individual must be responsible for, and master his or her life's path. All lessons learned along the way, will need to be remembered as the days grow short in the old dimension. But you have the keys, the awareness, the knowledge and wisdom, to ride the tidal wave successfully. We are with you.

May the healing light of goodness surround you, always,

Tibus

CHAPTER FORTY:
CAN WE DO IT?

This is Tibus. I come to you in love and light.

I wish to mention a ray of hope regarding this Change Times rollercoaster: Do you realize that 55% of Americans consider Nature to be sacred and/or spiritual! 19% of Americans say they practice meditation. And 63% of Americans feel the start of the new millennium should be a time for prayer and reflection rather than for fun and parties. 88% of Americans agree that "Protecting the environment will require most of us to make major changes in the way we live." 82% say that Americans buy and consume much more than they need.

These statistics are most encouraging, not only because of what they illustrate on the surface, but because of the momentum toward a leap in consciousness which these people will create as the actual Change Point occurs. The Change Point is the point at which the old frequency grows weak enough in its "hum," so that the new, higher frequency becomes the dominant "hum" of human consciousness.

The Renaissance following the Dark Ages, and the beginning of the 1960s "hippy" movement, are examples of two other steps forward in human history. These happened overnight and very few minds (individuals) were involved!

As The Renaissance dawned, we estimate that 8% of European individuals felt it was time for this change from the old, dark society. In the 1960s, very few Americans first felt the vibration of "The Age of Aquarius." This change snowballed overnight partially because of ceremonial drug use, which sadly, soon became general drug use; it is at this point that "The Age of Aquarius" was lost.

However, the basis of that 1960s leap forward was not drugs, it was simply an overnight half-step upward in evolution of the mass human consciousness.

Today, humanity faces a giant step (a leap) upward which will actually turn the page of reality and therefore also turn the page of dimension. It will be many times more difficult for individual minds to make than the previously mentioned "half-steps" upward. But, remember, it takes very few minds to affect a rise in consciousness. Is this not wonderful news to be aware of! So, such percentages as "55% of American people hold Nature sacred and/or spiritual," are really most encouraging. These statistics prove what we already know: Human Consciousness is Light Years ahead of its greedy, stupid governments' level of awareness.

HUMAN CONSCIOUSNESS: MOST ADAPTABLE IN THE UNIVERSE

The Human Consciousness is the most "unstable" of all consciousnesses of all the known races in the universe, did you know this? Human consciousness can change spontaneously, with relatively little motivation. It is highly flexible and adaptable. The mass consciousnesses of other universal races tend to be more stolid, less changeable, less whimsical. Their steps upward in spiritual evolution usually take a much longer time, not happening "overnight."

We of Future Human Consciousness who work within the Space/Time Intelligence, are sometimes kidded about our "quirky consciousness." My friends of other races tend to be more ponderous and studious, less spontaneous and whimsical. Earth's nature spirits also display a whimsical "quick silver" trait within their consciousness. This is a gift from our mother, The Earth. She is adaptable, changeable, and whimsical. Of course we (all her creations), reflect her, we are a part of her!

I should point out that although the Human Consciousness is "quirky," it always moves generally upward. It is built on past experience (history), and other elements which give a solid foundation. The Creator has endowed the Human Consciousness with the longing to return to that Creator. Thus "upward" is a given.

It is true that Earth is beginning to enter a "photon belt" as she journeys through the cosmos. This area of space does indeed have a higher rate of vibration in its subatomic particles than the space through which Earth has just traveled. These subatomic particles are, for all intents and purposes, consciousness particles.

We believe that each of us is a particle of consciousness in the Mind of God.

The Mind of God is turning into a new phase, looking toward The Dawn and emerging from a long, dark night. Soon The Mind of God will be in a new, enlightened mood! For these Change Times to be successfully survived, and for Earth to be able to fully turn the page of reality to a higher frequency of consciousness, an individual must be able to join this "change of mood" which will happen overnight.

It could happen that a planet would enter a higher vibration but that no individual on that planet could handle it. If this were the case, that race would be at an end. It would be doomsday for that species.

This will not be true of humanity; many of you are capable of making the leap in spiritual evolution, although the "overnight" aspect will be traumatic.

Enlightened people are not only capable, you can hardly wait for this leap in consciousness to occur. At last you will not feel like an alien. You have prepared yourself in many ways over the years.

We also have worked hard for this, hoping to make The Change Point as gentle and untraumatic as possible, and hoping to clarify questions regarding what is happening. To have knowledge is to be well prepared.

Remember, with **hope**, the door to the future is always open, whether wide open or a open just a crack. But, without hope, you slam the door shut, defeating yourself, before you arrive at the threshold.

May the healing light of goodness surround you, always

Tibus

CHAPTER FORTY-ONE:
THE BLUEPRINT FOR THE POINT OF CHANGE

(With thanks to a friend for sharing a personal reading)

This is Tibus. I come to you in love and light.

Often I have been asked whether The Change Point, which will occur in the first few years of The Healing Millennium, will thunder in dramatically or whether "The Change Moment" will take place without individuals on Earth even knowing it has happened. (Remember, "change" is perceived either just "before" or just "after," it cannot be perceived **during**, according to quantum physics theory).

Whether the Moment of Change is catastrophic or gentle, will depend on what intersect point on the Reality Continuum humankind manages to manifest.

The Reality Continuum concept is elaborated on in **Earth Changes Bible** because this concept is important to get across to everyone. I will give you an example: If a peaceful, relatively gentle "2" reality intersect point is reached on the Reality Continuum at the Moment of Change from the old dimension to the new, higher dimension, then that Change Moment will also be relatively peaceful, and not-discernible as it happens.

However, shortly afterward, you will realize that a new dimension has somehow dawned. You will know that something is different, and very much better, both within you, and outside of you. You will perceive that the human race has somehow skipped far ahead of where it was in thinking, feeling, and acting, than just the day before. A miracle will have happened.

As another example: If, at The Change Point, humankind has created an "8" on the Reality Continuum, all will be in chaos anyway. The climate will have gone much crazier than it is now, thus many natural catastrophes will be occurring along with bizarre "accidents," and acts of terrorism, with governments disintegrating.

The very Moment of Change would still not be perceivable to most. It would not be perceivable because of the surrounding chaos and threats to well-being. But certainly the moments leading up to it, would be chaotic and violent. After the Moment of Change, the chaos would still ensue for a brief while, and then it would seem that the sun has suddenly come out after an especially violent thunderstorm. Something wonderful would have have happened!

Only in the "Doomsday 10" intersect point on the Reality Continuum, does the sun (the light), not shine through, bringing a new world. If humanity creates a "10," no human will survive, and almost all life forms on Earth will be wiped out. But this alternate reality does not need to happen, does not need to be created!

The door is still wide open on what the exact reality will be when The Change occurs. This is why we must all work diligently for an enlightened future where life abounds, and the life force is held sacred.

As to the exact date of The Change Point, it will come in the first few years of the New Millennium, but the exact moment is also waiting for humankind to create it.

Various predictions of exact years have been made, but these depend on a specific "alternate reality" being created by humankind. In other words, humankind would have by that time created a "2," a "5" or an "8" for itself on the Reality Continuum. Each of these intersect points would contain a specific time for The Change Point to occur because of the specific circumstances of that particular reality. But you, my human friends, have yet to create your future reality! The door is still wide open to The Future.

In essence, every alternate reality imaginable will occur somewhere/somewhen. There are an infinite number of branch realities, not just ten as presented on our Reality Continuum. We use the number ten to make the concept comprehensible. Each branch reality exists in its own dimension, its own stage within the universal theater. You as an enlightened individual mind have the choice of choosing which "stage" on which you wish to appear/manifest. Which future reality do you wish to perceive and to participate in? Make your choice wisely, with the help of the greatest knowledge and wisdom available.

Because of what I have just explained, we will not set a year in which The Moment of Change will occur. Each of you have your own answer. It is very difficult to put such "fabric of reality" concepts into words and I sometimes think only a fool would embark on such a project. Suffice it to say that the branch of reality your mind will perceive and participate in, at the Moment of Change (and at any given moment), is up to you. Do you see why we are sure doomsday will not happen? Because your consciousness will never allow it to happen!

We can only go by what we have learned of the nature of reality, the history and behavior of the human race, the cosmic factors we know to exist at this time, and the condition of the Mother Planet.

After the Change Point, humans who are adaptable to the new, risen frequency of thinking, feeling, and acting, will begin perceiving other dimensional beings such as angels, nature sprites, gnomes, fairies, advanced celestrial beings, inner-dimensional beings, a whole universe-full of wondrous new beings to perceive and to know. Just imagine how astounding and beautiful this will be!

Of course, you will know the beings you wish to know. Just as with your fellow humans, you will choose those who are of goodness. You need not know the others; the choice is yours. Among these newly-perceived beings of goodness, will be many dear friends. The Veil will have been lifted! "Tunnel vision" has blocked humankind's full perception for aeons. This lifting of The Veil will be an event for cosmic celebration!

You will also have full conscious awareness of your parallel aspects (past and future lifetimes); suddenly you will have knowledge and memories which span The Ages. Personal memories, knowledge of historical events as they actually unfolded, and most important, a wondrous new comprehension of why you are **you**.

And, once and for all, you will fully perceive how life is eternal. There is no death! You will now remember, first hand, how the unique spark of life which is **you**, has gone on and on throughout The Ages, from lifetime to lifetime.

How will it happen that you will suddenly perceive and have knowledge of so many amazing beings and events? It will be as if you have just awakened from a long sleep, finding as you awaken, that entire worlds of perception, knowledge and experience are now with you, consciously. It will be as if they had been placed within your mind during your long sleep; your awakening will be as natural as awakening in the morning to a new day.

EACH INDIVIDUAL HAS A CHANGE POINT

Each individual goes through his or her own "change point" as well, in each life time. This is how each of us climbs the awareness ladder, one wrung at a time. And, once you achieve a certain level of consciousness, you never need to achieve it again.

Let's take your present lifetime as an example: You came here as a more sensitive, more enlightened soul than many around you. Thus you know that in past lives, you have reached a high level of consciousness. However, even in your present lifetime, it took years to come to the full conscious awareness of your enlightenment and high frequency of being.

"Enlightenment" is a funny commodity, because few individuals in the history of the universe, have been enlightened without realizing it. Usually, an individual does realize he or she is enlightened. Yet, it is a quality which automatically indicates humility - true humility. You do not have to "act humble," you truly are, knowing in your enlightenment that you are but a precious drop in the universal ocean.

The problem with this is that the daily world does not perceive your true nature and can tend to run over you, perceiving humble enlightenment and gentleness, for weakness. This illustrates the low frequency of the daily world; you realize this, but this knowledge does not keep you from being hurt and not fully valued.

In the current lifetimes which unfold for enlightened humans, during these Change Times on Earth, there is indeed a change point for each individual, too.

Many friends have written us, mentioning a particular moment when everything made sense, when suddenly they felt even more at home with the higher frequency and more alien in the daily world. The Light suddenly shone, in its full glory rather than in a half-perceived, half-felt way, as before. Suddenly, they perceived their true cosmic identity!

We have transmitted a number of messages pertaining to those of enlightenment becoming "more alien" in the unravelling daily frequency, and thus having more problems being a part of it. Yet, we have also commented how blessed and gifted is the enlightened person who is still functioning successfully, and with love, in the daily dimension.

Sadly, there are individuals who are indeed "alien" in the daily frequency who get lost in paranoia, drug or alcohol abuse, self pity, and/or extreme pessimism. Highly sensitive humans are like salmon swimming upstream. Who will arrive successfully into the New Dawn, and who will not survive the rapids, even though his urgency to reach the New Dawn is just as great? Often it seems that the object of this lifetime "game" on Earth is simply to hold onto your soul!

It comes down to individual spiritual strength and wisdom, and the amount of guidance which the enlightened person accepts from higher guides and fellow enlightened humans. If an individual becomes lost in the world of drugs, it numbs the pain of the daily dimension; however, other loving souls would advise him that drugs are not the answer, not the way to the New Dawn. He may well be dead before the Healing Millennium arrives. Even beyond loving guidance, this individual must find his own spiritual strength and wisdom. That is the ultimate answer for each of us.

Once you have experienced your own "change point" within the spirit quest which lies within your current lifetime, you will be well prepared for The Change Point which exists for the Mother Planet and for every individual, which we have described above. In this way you have a personal "change point" and a (near future) Change Point which you will share with all life on Planet Earth. Always remember: Find the God Spark within; it leads straight into the New Dawn.

May the healing light of goodness surround you always,

Tibus

CHAPTER FORTY-TWO:
BEFORE MEDITATIONS, THE TRUTH ABOUT CRYSTALS

This is Tibus. I come to you in love and light.

Since humankind's history on Earth began, crystals and gemstones have been linked with the mystical frontiers of outer space and with the spiritual frontiers of inner space. These include the search for higher consciousness and a new, enlightened reality.

We of Space/Time Intelligence have attempted to help individuals become aware of the wonderful powers of crystals and gemstones, which were made by the incredible creative force of the Mother Planet in very ancient times. These objects manifested from her inner heart and soul when all was young and pure.

As with other truths, we stress that the wisdom of "how to use crystals and gemstones" is not rooted exclusively in the scientific, nor is it rooted exclusively in the mystical. The wisdom of "how to use" is rooted in **both** the scientific perception and the mystical feeling. The sum of this "one plus one" concept equals much more than "two."

Why? Because when you perceive with your Whole Mind, rather than depending on only one side of your brain, you perceive a reality which is greater than you had imagined; this is how a leap in consciousness is accomplished.

When you work with a crystal, know its scientific reality. How was it formed? What specific kind of crystal is it? Where is it found? Is it plentiful or rare?

As you work with the same crystal, embrace its mystical aspects as well. What are its energies as you hold it? Are they warm and gentle? Or hot and very powerful? Does it have healing energy? Does its color feel right intuitively for the goal of the meditation you want to participate in? Is its shape helpful and dynamic? Is it linked to Egyptian energy? Or outer space, alien energy? Or ancient Celt energy? Does it have connections to your own star guardian? Does it connect to beings of Inner Earth?

Humankind has long made the mistake of expecting magic to happen from "outside," and therefore human beliefs are often very illogical and ignorant; this is where superstition takes over from authentic mysticism.

Consider the man who has a "lucky" rabbit's foot: First, why would possessing the foot of an unfortunate fellow creature, be lucky? Second, if this man is about to rob your home, should he be blessed with good luck? These questions reflect the ignorant concept that "luck comes from outside," and "luck is a commodity to be obtained," concepts which humanity has held during the Dark Millennium.

The truth is, an individual's consciousness must be involved with the object before "luck" can occur, and even more important, this individual's heart and soul must be of good intent. Otherwise, the use of objects to bring "luck," lead to a dark path, a path which is not consistently lucky at all. Sooner or later, this individual will be abandoned by his good luck, and bad luck will fill the vacuum.

In the Healing Millennium, humankind will finally realize that helpful objects such as crystals and gemstones, must only be used to forward the path of good intent.

Crystals and gemstones are helpmates which go far beyond the concept of "good luck." With them, the high frequency and beauty of your own mind is enhanced. Their energies contain the deepest creative power of the Mother Planet; these energies blend with your own.

You may feel that crystals and gemstones are alive. In fact, they do have a life force. This life force cannot be measured by brain wave readings, tests, or by most technical methods. However, crystals grow, they are children of Mother Earth just like all other life forms on the planet, they heal, they comfort, they assist in communication, interacting with the energies of "the other."

We say that crystals and gemstones have a "base of life." This is also true of giant boulders, stones, mountains, and hills. Mighty mountains, of course, have a mighty spirit which sometimes personifies herself. Volcanoes have an especially volatile and restless life force. Native Americans believe that all matter has a "manitou" (life base or life force). Their wisdom is profound.

Crystals and gemstones are found on planets throughout the galaxy and throughout the universe. Aboard our starships, we have crew members who are experts in this field, and often these experts will communicate telepathically with you when you are first working with a new crystal or gemstone. Be aware of this. They offer guidance and insight on the type of crystal you are working with, and regarding the nature of the specific crystal.

Gemstones and crystals vary greatly from one another, even if they are of the same kind. Their diversity is as infinite as other forms of life. It is fantastic to see a cross-section of crystals and gemstones from far distant worlds, sitting side by side with crystals and gemstones of Mother Earth. It is like the music of the spheres!

However, I must point out that some of the most beautiful crystals and gemstones in the universe, were created by Mother Earth. Her creative powers are absolutely incredible! The more worlds I visit, the more I know how beautiful and unique my own mother planet, is! You do not have to use crystals or gemstones in meditations, my friend. That is up to you. Some enlightened people find that the use of an object only gets between them and their Creator, similar to religious objects which seem antiquated and/or not useful. Other enlightened individuals find that their specially chosen crystals and gemstones work miracles at times, and greatly enhance their meditation and spiritual work at all times.

We will give you several very special meditations as a conclusion to this book, which use crystals or gemstones.

WHEN TO USE THESE SPECIAL MEDITATIONS

The meditations which I have chosen to give you as the Dark Millennium fades, turning toward the dawn of the Healing Millennium, will help you raise The Seven Rays of your own consciousness, and also help raise The Seven Rays of Human Consciousness.

These special meditations will help you to heal yourself or another (including your animal friends), help you in guiding your life to a positive and productive path, and help you in contacting higher beings, including your own star guardian. They will help you into a new, more positive dimension. You have merely to set the purpose and goal of the meditation before you start; set it with your mind and soul.

If you need to concentrate and focus, write down the purpose and goal of your meditation. You may even want to write down the goal of your upcoming meditation seven times on a sheet of paper; this will solidify your goal into this reality.

These special meditations can also be used in all-encompassing efforts to cleanse and heal Mother Earth, or any part of her, such as a river or lake which is badly polluted. These meditations can be applied to any of the problems we have mentioned in this book; we urge you to use them to help Mother Earth's wild creatures especially. These can be used to send healing energy to the rainforest or to help fortify the ozone layer which is Earth's immune system.

In the monthly newsletter Diane and I write, we give specific dates when other light workers will be meditating, praying, and working, to cleanse and heal our very troubled planet. This newsletter, **The Star Network Heartline,** has been going without fail for sixteen years. We know when enlightened people join energies together, they become many times more powerful; this has been our experience throughout the years as we perform vital spiritual work through the **Star Network.**

We hope that each and every reader of this book will join our **Star Network,** or at least ask us for a free sample of **The Heartline** newsletter, so that you can join with our many friends in one of our cleansing/healing efforts. These benefit us as individuals as well as helping Mother Earth.

We are very proud of our spiritual accomplishments and will continue to work tirelessly as a united network, in the crisis days ahead. We absolutely know we are making a positive difference!

Our publication, **The Change Times Quarterly,** also gives vital information on emergencies around the world and sets specific dates to upgrade reality through the power of our united minds and souls. Not only do we help raise the frequency, but we raise our own Seven Rays when we participate in such spiritually dynamic efforts. Details on how to participate will be given at the close of this book.

May the healing light of goodness surround you, always,

Tibus (with Diane's in-put)

CHAPTER FORTY-THREE:
SEVEN MUSICAL NOTES FOR SEVEN RAINBOW RAYS

Musical note: Do Color: Red Chakra: **Root**
Which of the Seven Rays of Human Consciousness: **Man's way of thinking, feeling, acting toward Mother Earth**

Musical note: Re Color: Orange Chakra: Sacral (genital)
Which of the Seven Rays of Human Consciousness: **Man's way of thinking, feeling, acting toward others**

Musical note: Mi Color: Yellow Chakra: Solar Plexus
Which of the Seven Rays of Human Consciousness: **Man's way of thinking, feeling, acting toward other life forms who share his world**

Musical note: Fa Color: Green Chakra: Heart
Which of the Seven Rays of Human Consciousness: **Man's Way of thinking, feeling, acting toward his own spirituality, his soul, and his future**

Musical note: So Color: Blue Chakra: Throat
Which of the Seven Rays of Human Consciousness: **Man's way of thinking, feeling, acting toward the Great Unknown and alien life**

Musical note: La Color: Indigo Chakra: Brow
Which of the Seven Rays of Human Consciousness: **Man's way of thinking, feeling, acting toward his mental and physical development**

Musical note: Ti Color: Violet Chakra: Crown
Which of the Seven Rays of Human Consciousness: **Man's way of thinking, feeling, acting toward his Creator**

In the Healing Millennium, the field of "the seven sacred energies" will at last be unified! Unified will be the <u>musical scale</u> of the human "hum," as it is raised an octave. Tonal frequencies are vital in the composition of the molecules of any dimension. Just remember how important tonal communication is in **Close Encounters of the Third Kind.** Into this unified field, will come the <u>cosmic color spectrum</u>, which manifests the rainbow. Rainbows always symbolize hope and a bright new day, the discovery of treasure at the end of a long journey. The seven colors are also a vital ingredient of the molecules of a any dimension.

Then, unified into this field will be humankind's <u>chakra system</u> which carries every individual's psychic and spiritual energy. It is within this system that the "hum" will be raised an octave, the colors intensified.

Planet Earth also has seven different chakras; within Earth, these chakras are called ley lines. There are seven different kinds.

And so, with this unified field, spiritual evolution will take place!

MEDITATION FOR SERENITY AND FOR GUIDANCE:

Use a crystal for this meditation which catches the color of the spectrum when you hold it in the light. The source of light may be either the sun or the flame of a candle. Clear you mind of daily cares and problems. Concentrate on the simple beauty of the light shining through your crystal. Spend time dangling the crystal so that it catches the optimum prism affect.

Now, surround yourself with golden light of good intent and imagine that golden light mingling with the crystal's spectrum of colors. Doing this will help you further clear your mind of daily problems and thoughts. Take seven deep breaths and thoroughly relax yourself. Feel serenity and peace. Do not try for profound thoughts or revelations, just **be.**

Feel the energies flowing through your Crown and Brow Chakras, feel your third eye area receiving a rush of colorful energy, as if the colors of the crystal had flowed into your consciousness. This is divine energy traveling on the wings of the crystal's colors, coming to heal and rejuvenate you.

150

Now, concentrate on your crystal as it shines in the light and see which color within the crystal stands out most to you at the moment. You catch glimpses of all colors of the rainbow but one color will intuitively come to you in particular at this time. Remember which color this is, because a little later on, you will see what guidance was given to you through this particular color.

Move your crystal a bit and simply enjoy the beauty of it. Allow it to clear your mind and heart of problems. Feel wonder and joy at the natural phenomenon of the colors of the spectrum and of the crystal with its many traits of "being alive."

Visualize a rainbow with a giant-size crystal in the middle of it. Allow your mind to play with similar visualizations using crystals and rainbows.

Allow this time of meditation to continue as long as you wish. It need not go on for a long time, just doing what we have described will be restful and healing.

MESSAGES IN COLOR, AND ANIMAL TOTEMS

When you are done with your actual meditation, remember what color came to you in particular. Check to see what chakra it relates to in our listing above. This should give you a hint as to what area of your body may need extra attention; perhaps you need to obtain an herb or vitamin which is helpful to this part or system of your body. Perhaps you need to pay more attention to the health of this aspect of your body.

Or, perhaps the chakra which is located in this part of your body, needs more attention spiritually.

Using the color which comes to you in meditation or at a spiritual moment, can be used as animal totems are used. It usually does not indicate anything terribly earth-shaking but simply offers guidance and spiritual in-put which the enlightened individual finds helpful. Use the clue it gives you to help guide you at that moment.

We highly recommend studying the concept of animal totems, too Every individual has an animal totem (mammal, bird, reptile, amphibian or insect), who spiritually stays with him or her for a long period of time; however, your animal totem almost never stays with you all your life. As your life's phases change, so does your animal totem. A person with shamanistic abilities can help you determine which animal is your personal totem at present.

Animal totems are also helpful on a spontaneous basis. If you are on a hike and spy a fox, what spiritual message does The Fox hold for you? Should you be more clever in your current dealings? Should you not be an open book to everyone? Is there an aspect of your present lifetime which you are not perceiving clearly? Perhaps you should give this area of your life some specific thought before a crisis arises. All of this and more, can be brought to your attention because a fox crossed your path. This is what the universe is trying to say to you!

CHAPTER FORTY-FOUR:
MEDITATIONS TO RAISE THE SEVEN RAYS

CHANNELING CRYSTAL MEDITATION

By "channeling crystal," we mean a pointed, elongated crystal which is either leaded crystal (similar in shape to those which hang from chandeliers), or a natural crystal "point" straight from Mother Earth.

We prefer natural crystals because they are from our beloved Mother Planet; we prefer the infinite diversity which Mother Nature invests in her creations instead of the "all the same" items which humans produce.

However, there is nothing wrong or detrimental in using leaded crystal, usually manufactured in Austria. A few years ago, the rumor traveled through New Age circles that leaded crystal was somehow negative or dangerous. The motivation behind this rumor was probably financial, because people threw out their Austrian crystals and bought expensive new natural crystals. Among my meditation crystals, there are several cherished Austrian crystals.

The truly important ingredient in meditation is **you.** Use whatever crystal you feel is good for you, whatever crystal you feel helps you most.

The source of light for the meditation we are about to embark upon, may be the light from the sun, or starlight and/or moonlight; meditations done outside in the nighttime can be very energizing and dynamic.

First, find a comfortable position. If you are doing this meditation outdoors instead of using the sunlight through a window, be sure you are dressed warmly enough (or coolly enough, on a summer day). You want to be able to forget your physical body and its woes.

Clear your mind of daily cares. Take seven deep breaths. Relax deeply and thoroughly. Surround yourself with the golden light of good intent.

Hold your crystal in the light source, or if it is on a chain, allow it to dangle in the light. Notice the rainbow which is created as light travels through the beautiful crystal. Allow the light to continue traveling through the crystal for a moment, this will energize it. Obviously if you are doing this on a starlight night, there will be less light and the "twinkle" effect of stars and crystal will be your light source.

Now, lift your head skyward, even if you are indoors. Surrender yourself to The Creator Spirit. Feel serenity pour in. Close your eyes while your head is still tilted skyward and feel God's love washing over your face and into your deepest being. You are being cleansed, you are being given new strength. Now, open your eyes and look at your crystal. How like the stars it is! Both have unique mystical energy and an alien intelligence. Both shine, both are vessels of the light.

Continue concentrating on your channeling crystal. This shape of crystal is particularly effective in helping you contact higher beings. Sometimes you will be delightfully surprised to find a message (a sentence or several sentences), forming in your mind. They have been transmitted to you from your spiritual family or your own star guardian. Other times, you may find a scenario has formed in your mind which has a symbolic message for you.

Other times, you will receive only a word or two, or perhaps nothing in the way of actual verbal message or coherent scenario or visualization. If this is the case, do not feel frustrated or ignored. Continue your meditations, similar to the one we have just given you, whenever you can.

Don't try to force the issue of coherent communication or contact. It will happen, but a watched pot never seems to boil, so relax and enjoy the mystical beauty and quality of your channeling crystal as it shines in the natural light. Enjoy the simple spirituality of the meditation experience. This is "enough!"

Remember that meditation is the gift of opening the mind and simply being; meditation is not a state of mind where you force yourself to think up the experience. Simply be serene, be relaxed and open, be quiet. Keep your mind quiet.

When you do receive a word, a sentence, a scenario, a concept, from "outside," you may not be able to differentiate it from your own higher thoughts, especially at first. Most times, contact does not come into your mind in a big, thundering voice. Higher beings do not want to upset you with a bizarre and outlandish experience like that, and it simply isn't what "contact" is really like.

It may take some time for you to learn to know when a message comes from "outside," instead of from inside your own mind. But, this is alright, there is usually no rush. It is important to read the symbolism within any message and to consider the meaning deeply. Contact with positive beings is gentle, loving, and gives you a serene, secure feeling. Once in a while this may not be true if your higher friends have an urgent and important message for you.

We have given you a basic meditation to be done with a channeling crystal. It involves the simplicity of the crystal and natural lighting, be it the sun, moon, or stars. This meditation will assist you in simply "being" so that the optimum universal energies will flow into you, opening you for contact.

This meditation does not involve a lot of words you must say, or detailed ritual steps you must take. After all, when all is said and done, the key and the power will come not from an elaborate ritual, but from **you.**

GEMSTONE HEALING MEDITATION

This meditation may be used to help heal yourself or another individual, including an animal. It can also be used to heal a specific area in nature, such as a polluted stream or a forested area which has just been cut; also, this meditation may also be used to heal Gaia, the living spirit of our entire Mother Planet.

We have found the gemstone Moldavite particularly helpful in this meditation. You may use whatever gemstone has warm, good, healing energies which you can relate to and feel as you hold your gemstone in your hand.

Individuals vary as to which kind of gemstone's energies they connect to; even though a gemstone like Moldavite has especially powerful healing energies, you as an individual might prefer a simple Agate or Lapis Lazuli which Edgar Cayce recommended. Or, you might have a favorite individual gemstone which you know has proven healing powers, and you might not feel these powers from other gemstones of the same kind.

In other words, the choice of gemstone is yours and it is a very personal choice.

If you are looking for guidance as to which gemstone to try in healing meditations, we do recommend Moldavite or Connemara Marble.

Moldavite is a translucent green gemstone, the only known gemstone from outer space. Moldavite fell over what is now Czechoslovakia about 14.8 million years ago. Scientists still argue whether tektites such as Moldavite are true meteorites or whether they were formed through fusion with earthly materials.

In ancient times, Moldavite was used for amulets and talisman; it is a rare gemstone not found in abundance. Moldavite has an extremely high spiritual vibration and can help the individual raise his or her Seven Rays of Consciousness; it helps accelerate the vibration of the spiritual path, and in the process, has wondrous healing energies. When most people hold it, they feel great warmth and even a tingle. Moldavite connects especially to the Heart, Brow (Third Eye) and Crown Chakras. In legend, Moldavite is linked to the Holy Grail which is said to have been adorned with a magical emerald stone which fell from the heavens.

Connemara Marble comes only from the West of Ireland. It can be purchased in Ireland but is difficult to find elsewhere. When I lived in Ireland, I offered deep green Connemara Marble to my friends and subscribers, and many of us had wonderful healing success with it.

Other gemstones with which our **Star Network** (and myself), have had excellent healing success, include Rose Quartz, Amethyst Quartz, and Lapis Lazuli.

If you are having a healing meditation to help yourself, do this meditation lying down in a comfortable position. Meditations are always dynamic if done out in Mother Nature, but if you are healing yourself, be comfortable! You may want to stay inside simply for privacy and if the weather is not ideal.

Of course if you are healing an area of Mother Nature, or the entire living spirit of the planet, it is best to be outdoors if possible.

If you are healing another individual, have them lie down; you will be in a comfortable sitting position. If you are healing an animal friend, get them as quiet and relaxed as possible.

Take seven deep breaths and relax. Allow the golden light of good intent to wash over this entire healing session, enhancing and blessing this endeavor.

Hold your healing gemstone in both your hands, giving the gemstone your warmth and energies, and allowing its warmth and energies to flow into you. Mingle with the gemstone, become one with it.

Now, place it on the area which needs healing, whether it is within yourself, or within another individual. (Obviously the position you are in depends on what area you are healing). The gemstone should be touching the skin, not trying to work through clothing. If possible, hold both your hands over the gemstone as it sits on the area in need of healing; holding one hand on top of the gemstone will also be effective.

If you are healing an area of water in Mother Nature, sit on the bank or shore. If you are healing an area of Mother Nature on land, sit in the middle of this area if possible. At least be in physical contact with some part of the damaged area. If you are healing an area of Mother Nature, or Gaia herself, you will continue holding your healing gemstone, clasped in both hands throughout the meditation. Hold your hands close to your body, preferably near the Solar Plexus and Heart Chakras.

Now say or feel these words, "Be cleansed. Be purified. Be healed!" Repeat these words two times (a total of three times) without stopping.

Let your words become a mantra of healing energy; feel what you are saying as a concept rather than mere words. Aim this deeply felt concept right at the area to be healed.

Let the power of these words (the concept for which they stand), mingle with your gemstone, making it a booster station for your healing power. It will enhance your healing energies and work its own little miracle as well.

Be silent for a moment. Look at your gemstone and visualize it glowing and humming; it is like a powerful, magical "booster station" which sends your cleansing, purifying, healing energies right to the area in need!

After this momentary break, again repeat, "Be cleansed. Be purified. Be healed." Say this three times without stopping. Aim your words/energies at the area in need of healing.

If you are healing the whole planet, visualize the world, or have a globe in front of you. Visualize Earth's clouds, oceans, and land masses, similar to what astronauts in space see. If you have a photo taken of Earth from space, this is good to use, too. Or, you can send your healing energies for the entire Mother Planet to a special power spot which you have picked out in nature. You can send these healing energies to the vegetation, the air, the ground, the wildlife of a powerful spot, and Gaia as a whole will receive it.

To complete this meditation, say, "Be cleansed, be purified, Be healed," three more times after a moment's rest in which you feel the serenity of silence. Look at your gemstone again if you wish and see what thought comes to you, from it.

Your cleansing, purifying, healing mantra should be spoken a total of "three times three." That is, say it three times, then rest. Say it another three times, then rest. And say it a final three times.

To conclude this gemstone healing meditation, send love, peace, and serenity into the universe, and say, "I now conclude this meditation until next time."

You can do this "three times three" meditation with your favorite healing gemstone as often as you wish.

CHAPTER FORTY-FIVE:
A FINAL WORD FROM DIANE

It is amazing in a frightening way: These days of Earth Changes are unfolding just as Tibus and his co-workers predicted they would. That was sixteen years ago when I first started channeling their messages.

At the time, I really didn't know what their goal was or if they even had a goal. I knew Tibus and his friends were beings of good intent but aside from that, I was one of their biggest skeptics. I had to put my skepticism aside when I channeled them, but I found it helpful to take their existence with a grain of salt as I went about my everyday life. This was partly because I realized what was happening had enormous implications, and my skepticism and nonchalance helped me deal with this fact.

Always, there has been humor between Tibus and myself, and usually between myself and other channeled friends. Tibus especially is used to being taken lightly by me; I believe this light hearted approach has helped us keep our conduit of communication wide open for years now. The last thing Tibus wants to be is a pompous stuffed shirt who feels he is better than everyone else. Always, Tibus stresses equality, and I like the old boy for that.

Also, my skepticism when I started out those sixteen years ago, helped me keep my own beinghood, rights, and opinions, so as not to become a mindless "true believer" who did not weigh the worth of words I channeled. I did in fact consider every word I channeled, and judged it for its intelligence and goodness. Only then did I write it down.

This still holds true today. If a concept I am channeling does not ring true, I re-examine it, re-opening the channels and asking for clarification. Usually the problem is that I have written it down in a topsy turvy thought process; I work on the concept like any craftsperson works on an object, clarifying what is being transmitted, and being sure I write it down with accuracy.

As I write the conclusion to this book, the news headlines of the day echo with eerie accuracy, the predictions which I received from our higher friends, sixteen years ago. People have lost faith in politicians. Society is chaotic, with computers running our lives. The economy is not what we are told it is, and the Asian economy in particular, is in ruins. The climate is crazy, ice is melting at the poles. You know the list of Earth Changes well, so I won't repeat them.

The point is, when I first channeled such warnings and predictions sixteen years ago, I didn't perceive the entire reality which would unfold. I didn't know there was a plan. But Tibus and his friends obviously did have knowledge of the reality we would be facing at the turn of the millennium, and they did (and do!) have a plan.

That plan is to help those of us who are capable, into a brand new dimension. The page is turning, and if we are adaptable and can raise our Seven Rays of Consciousness, we will exist on that new page of reality.

The frequency of our consciousness will be able to function in the next octave.

"Do, re, mi, fa, so, la, ti, do." Start at the first "do," and then travel up the scale, singing your life's song in the new, higher octave! If you go step by step, through the stages of spiritual exploration and experience, it is not a difficult move to make.

Our higher friends can guide us, and they really knock themselves out trying to do this! But ultimately, it is up to each individual to sing his or her own life's song. It is up to you to raise your consciousness and move into the Healing Millennium.

This has never happened before in human history, not to this degree. What a challenge! And, how exciting!

Be in the Healing Millennium! Visualize yourself there. The Mind of God will be in a new enlightened phase, the molecules of consciousness which are you, will be of a higher order, a higher octave. Unified. Whole. This is going to happen. **Be** - there!

I hope that you will join our **Star Network** immediately and participate in our united effort to heal the planet and to raise the spiritual frequency. Participating helps each of us as well as our Mother Planet, to make it into the future reality, and to flourish there.

We also have special days in which our friends on high, heal and rejuvenate us through their wondrous and powerful energies, so we can continue our mission.

I wish to give special thanks to my friends of **The Star Network** for their encouragement and patience regarding this effort, and for their abiding love and support throughout the years. With individuals like these, there can be no doubt that Mother Earth and her inhabitants will soon celebrate the bright new dawn of the Healing Millennium.

Diane Tessman
P.O. Box 352
St. Ansgar, Iowa 50472

Artist: Carol Ann Rodriguez

PERSONAL COUNSELING BY DIANE
PRIVATE CHANNELING BY TIBUS

Receive precious guidance and psychic information from Diane Tessman and her star guardian, Tibus. This is a written channeling you will cherish all your life, which will also give you an invaluable road map in the frightening days ahead. These readings have been transformational for thousands of people!

Feel free to write explaining your specifics when you request your reading. Specify if you wish to place emphasis on counseling by Diane or on telepathic communication with Tibus, through Diane. If you do not specify, Diane and Tibus will share in-put into your personal, private counseling which will be a minimum of five single-spaced type-written pages - just for you!

Diane and Tibus will work with your past and future lifetimes, financial, love, sex, health, relationship problems, impart your blueprint for the upcoming Earth changes, help in contacting your personal guardian, practical counseling for difficulties encountered in the world (improving "luck"), and more! $100.00

* We can accept a very limited number of students. After your first channeling, we will consider this if you wish.

THE CHANGE TIMES QUARTERLY by Diane

Tessman, is published 4 times a year with urgent transmissions from Tibus, Veritan, Amethysta, other members of the Space/Time Intelligence. Current global crisis are explained, crucial information is given! **Find out the truth with facts which are censored from the regular news media. CTQ can literally help you survive the times ahead!** Get the real story on cancer, AIDS, government/negative alien conspiracy, the break up of Antarctica, predictions of floods, quakes, info available no where else on UFOs & upcoming meetings between millions of aliens & humans, & much more! Subscription is $45.00 p/year (4 issues). Current sample copy, $5.00. Write today!

THE STAR NETWORK HEARTLINE, written

monthly by Diane & Tibus for 16 years, treasured by thousands of Light Workers. **The Heartline** gives the dates of our Star Network's Healing Days which are raising the frequency. Join us, please! Don't miss out, you are not alone! $30 per year. <u>Write for sample copy FREE!</u>

Send $1.00 for <u>EARTH CHANGES CATALOG</u> with wonderful, uplifting videos by Diane, incredible channeled manuscripts, moldavite, crystal quartz, gemstones, and much more!

Diane Tessman, P.O. Box 352, St. Ansgar, Iowa 50472

Powerful Secrets That Will Change Your Life–Now!

■ Now is the time to turn yourself into a more desirable individual capable of obtaining all that you personally desire.

■ Angelic beings exist in other dimensions all around us and are willing to provide assistance any time we call upon them.

■ We all survive death and go on to a happier existence in the afterlife.

■ A powerful symbolic cross may be all we need to protect us.

reminded me that crystals have always been respected for their healing and spiritual powers, and that eons ago even great prophets such as Moses used gems in a special breastplate when they wished to speak directly to God.

MY NEED TO HELP OTHERS

Shortly after finding the cross my life took a dramatic turn. I opened a church and started offering personal advice directed to me from "invisible friends."

In no time I was off welfare, I had purchased a home people started writing from around the world wanting to know about my experiences and what I had learned my experiences with "them."

One thing my angelic friends indicated is that it is within the realm of possibility for everyone living on this planet to receive whatever YOU desire. They added that in addition to positive thinking it would be a great help if people carried with them a simple crystal cross like the one I had found. They also indicated that those carrying this replica have a better chance of surviving the coming End Times. In effect, the cross acts like a "two for one" magnet to attract goodness and positive vibrations.

I looked all over the world and discovered a manufacturer in Austria who had a limited supply of such crosses and they were offered to me at a reasonable cost so that I might be able to give away one to anyone who desired to receive a copy of my personal testimony in the form of a book titled, *The Transformation.* I must have dispensed over ten thousand of these crystal crosses until I could no longer obtain them from my source. A damper was placed upon my being able to help those who were requesting my assistance. I felt disappointed and hurt.

However, I have come across another source who is able to supply me with the necessary crystal crosses that I missed so badly.

NOT FOR SALE

In another vision, I was admonished not to sell the cross if at all possible, But, how, was I to finance such an expensive operation (these crosses do cost a good sum to obtain). I have thus decided to offer free once again these crystal crosses to those who would like to read my latest work.

YOUR PASSPORT TO HEAVEN

Many of the people whom I have counseled have been deeply grieved by the passing of someone they love—with either a family member or a close friend. They want in many cases to be assured that there is an after life—that our soul does continue on after our physical body has gone.

In my latest book YOUR PASSPORT TO HEAVEN I share my personal experiences and what I have learned from my guides when it comes to "going to a higher place" when we die.

But this is not—by any means—a depressing or sad account ...not in any way for it offers us all hope that we will share a place next to the universal creator when our time is up here on Earth.

Some of the questions I try to answer in this book include:

♥ Exactly where is Heaven?

♥ How can a person be assured of going there when they die?

♥ Is there more than one place of existence in the afterlife?

♥ Will my loved ones—and pets—be there to greet and confront me?

♥ Can we communicate with the "next world" now (some investigators claim they have recently picked up pictures on their

TV sets from those they miss so much)?

♥ How close is Heaven to Earth and is it possible to visit there before we die?

♥ Can the dead pick up the telephone and speak with the living from the "other side" (one celebrity told us a very interesting personal story which we relate).

BE A WINNER—IN THIS LIFE AND THE NEXT!

If you wish to receive my free cross of crystal and learn more about Heaven please take the next few moments to fill out the necessary information so that my book and gift can be sent to you immediately. I can almost guarantee that you will find a most rewarding change will come about once you have had the opportunity to carry or wear the cross of crystal and experience the accompanying angelic-like qualities that radiate from within the very soul of this great instrument of power that offers personal prosperity, success and individual protection. In addition, I firmly believe you will enjoy and benefit greatly from my latest book which needs to be read in these changing times in history to lift our spirits and radiate hope into our hearts.

God speed to
you one & all—
Diane